Ifalade Ta'Shia Asanti and Azaan Kamau

LETTERS

TO MY

BULLY

EDITED BY
IFALADE TA'SHIA ASANTI & AZAAN KAMAU

"Being resilient was something that I didn't realize I was when I was in junior high & high school. From being called "ugly", "fat-so", "retarded", "stupid", to being taunted, teased and mean-mugged...it lowered my self-esteem. But I somehow found a way to not allow it to dwell in my spirit. I channeled those energies through reading & writing, and enjoying old school music. Indeed, being bullied bothered me, but after learning resilience,
I refused to let it grab a hold of me".

Author Tiffany C. Pace a.k.a. Poetic Old Soul ©

Glover Lane Press
A Division of Azaan Kamau Media
921 Molino Ave Suite A
Long Beach, CA 90804

Editor: Ifalade Ta'Shia Asanti
Editor: Azaan Kamau
Guest Editor: Audrey F. Liggins & PER Services
Book Design: Azaan Kamau

First Published by Glover Lane Press August 2012

For information on book signings, bulk orders, or press info
contact:
Glover Lane Press at gloverlanepress@gmail.com or
tashia@tashiaasanti.com

For titles by Glover Lane Press or Ifalade Ta'Shia Asanti
Please visit: www. Tashiaasanti.com and/or
www.gloverlanepress.webs.com

ISBN-13: 978-0615582160 (Glover Lane Press)

ISBN-10: 0615582168
The Mission of Glover Lane Press is to Uplift, Empower and
Elevate the Masses

DEDICATION-AZAAN

I dedicated this book to my favorite Italian Marie Lutz, who taught me at a very young age that bullying should never be accepted or tolerated! This book of amazing letters is also dedicated to everyone that was ever bullied by somebody. To everyone that was bullied to death!

I especially dedicate this literary work to the beautiful transgender 19 year old Henry Hilliard Jr. a.k.a. Shelly Moore, and also to Shelly Moore's mother Ms. Lyniece Nelson.

Shelly had been missing for several weeks. Shelly's burned torso was found on the side of I-94 on October 23, 2011.

Shelly, you were absolutely beautiful, independent, kind and compassionate.

You will be missed.

I dedicate this book you, Shelly

Ifalade Ta'Shia Asanti and Azaan Kamau

ACKNOWLEDGMENTS-AZAAN

Thank you to my African Ancestors who guide and light my path. Thank you so very much to my big sis Desiree who supports me no matter what! Thank you to my mother Madlyn! Thank you for supporting me in all that I do. I love you! Thank you to Marie Lutz who taught me volumes by using herself as an example of humanity. Thank you Marie! Salima MaSud for your unconditional love and words of wisdom! Very special thanks to Ifalade Ta'Shia Asanti, whose teaching, guidance, and utter patience keeps me strong and mindful. Thank you to my dear friend Pat Lamis who *always* has my back! Thank you so much to the amazing multi-talented Actor, Poet, and Activist Robert LaSardo. Thank you to the The Henderson Sisters, they are too cute! Tim'm T. West for Red Dirt Music Publishing, TreZure and Smut Stud!, Jacquelyn Kennedy of the ground breaking Dewberries Boutique & Cultural Center, Kergan Edwards-Stout, Jessica Knapp, Lindsay Delong, Scott Taylor, Ed Madden, Rachel Towns, Tom Rastrelli, Jeremy Halinen, Ona Marae, the absolutely amazing DJ Nova Jade, J.C. Odasor, Gary Dixon, Denina Taylor, Spine-tingling best-selling author of The Temp, A.H. Scott,   the multifaceted Yolanda Arroya Pizarro, writer triumphant victor, Rebecca Raymer April Mae Berza, R. D. Wylder, Aser Peleg, to Kevin Mc Lellen…thank you for great conversation, Shannon Pacaoan, Amy La Coe, THANK YOU Tammy L. R. Young for your much needed love and editorial support! Congratulations to Tina Cates on your upcoming books Kitty Kat Letters & Spoken Wordz. Thank you to Neil Ellis Ortis, My Twin Katrina, thank you to my amazing niece who is the hardest working woman in Texas Jazar F. Kahr! Thank you to Bill Klemm, Rab Marlow, the passionate Cheryl Lewis Beverly, Tiffany C. Pace-Poetic Old Soul, Christopher Soden, Monica Anderson and, last but not least, Audrey F. Liggins! Thank You Audrey!

ACKNOWLEDGMENTS-IFALADE TA'SHIA ASANTI

To my Grandsons, Khalil, Lavelle, Kaelan and Malcolm—may you never bear the stripes of a bully. To my daughter, Danielle, whose bullies I would take on one by one, even now. To my brother Francis, for standing up to my bully and making sure the whole school knew what they were in for if anybody ever put their hands on me again. For all the young lives that were lost as a result of the lack of compassion, tolerance for social and cultural difference. May all God's children be protected, honored and loved. If no one else does, I love you…Ta'Shia

Table of Contents

PREFACE

Kergan Edwards-Stout

Turning Terror into Triumph

I still remember the terror I felt, every time I approached the soccer field. It was junior high, a difficult time for all, but for me, it felt even worse.

I'd always known I was gay. Even in kindergarten, just looking at Jeff Hayward's smile would make me happy, providing boundless energy which would propel me throughout the day. And I knew, intrinsically, that it was alright to feel this way—to love other boys—as everything about it felt completely natural and unforced.

But in junior high, things changed. What I had seen as natural and good suddenly was being labeled as abnormal—detestable, even. While I caught flak from many, and would dodge the verbal taunts at lunchtime, the worst offenders turned out to be fellow members of my soccer team. You'd think that, as team members wanting to win, Johnny Shea and Mike Trautman would have supported me, but every day I would face a barrage of insults, some veiled, some not, as we sat on the sidelines.

"Faggot" was spit towards me, with the kind of bile and hatred I could both feel and see plain on their faces. Whispers and dirty looks on a daily basis would continually unnerve me, affecting both my sense of self, as well as my performance on the field. These questions about my masculinity hovered over me, and I would feel physically ill at the thought of another practice or game.

Somehow, however, I survived. I just kept putting one foot in front of the other, keeping myself at a distance from all who would harm me. And, as the phrase goes, it did get better.

In high school, while I went on to be active in theatre and academics, Johnny Shea and Mike Trautman continued to rise socially, becoming the big men on campus that I'd always longed to be. In our junior year, Johnny was even voted onto the homecoming king's court, and as he took to the field, flashing his charming smile, all I could see was the sneer on his lips when he turned and looked my way.

A short time later, during summer break, word came that Johnny had tried to commit suicide and was in a coma. No one knew what had happened, and he eventually returned to school our senior year, but I could sense something in him had changed.

The following summer, I got another call. Johnny had tried again to kill himself, hanging a noose from the rafters in his garage, and had succeeded. He'd also left behind a note, writing that although he did not like girls, he did not want to like boys.

As difficult as it may be to see at the time, our tormentors often have their own issues, to which we are not privy. Whether they are secretly gay, or filled with self-doubt, or are simply taught at a young age to hate, their anger and animosity is fueled not by us, but from something deep within.

I later learned that Johnny's buddy Mike had a younger brother who came out as gay, and at our high school reunion, Mike sought me out, attempting to make amends for his past actions.

We all grow. We all have the capacity to change. The question becomes, how do we deal with abuse? Do we let our tormentors corrupt us? Do we turn into them? Do we hide? Or do we call out abuse for what it is, and insist that our lives not fall victim to it?

If you are experiencing harassment, in any form, take advantage of the resources in our community. Seek out a counselor or therapist. Find a support group, in person or online. And make sure that you use the opportunity to better yourself and those around you.

Take control. Don't let the moment define you. Let it be you that define the moment.

We can be so much better, if only we try.

Ifalade Ta'Shia Asanti and Azaan Kamau

FOREWORD

Ifalade Ta'Shia Asanti

It is my belief that Azaan Kamau's vision for this anthology was inspired by God. I say this because I believe that the hope that children, teens and adults impacted by bullying might read this anthology and know that they are not alone, that there is hope for their healing and empowerment beyond the trauma, is truly God's will.

I say this also because I too am a survivor of bullying. I was hated and picked on because my hair was wavy and because I had what they called, "good hair," whatever that is. Any hair that covers our head is good. I was also told I talked like a, "white girl." While I had no idea then that speaking good and proper English was restricted to a particular race of people, I did my best to defy those stereotypes. I wore my hair in a afro and learned how to break a few verbs.

I even taught myself to pretend I couldn't read and that I couldn't pronounce big words. It worked for a while until I invited my friends to my home which was filled with fine art, antique furniture and tons of books. Once again, I was too rich, smart, classy and had too good of a hair texture to be a part of the girl clique at my school.

My bullies chased me home from school under threat of physical harm. One bully took an ink pen and wrote on my face. I told my mother and she did what all school teacher moms did, she made an appointment with the principal of the school and contacted the child's mother. I wanted her to be like my friend Marilyn's family and get the entire family to line up on the lawn with baseball bats and frying pans to beat up my bully. She chose a civil solution. Fortunately, I told my brother and he went up to the school and let some kids know what time it was if they EVER put their hands on me again. I love you big brother!

Thanks to some wonderful teaching staff and school counselors, a new group of friends and a big brother who had a lot of courage,

I survived my bullies with minimal scars. My mother's intervention also let my bullies know they'd be held accountable at home for their actions. Some of the contributors to this anthology weren't as fortunate as I was. But the fact that they've written their story and lived to tell that story, speaks volumes about their courage, resilience and strength to overcome the effects of bullying.

Stereotyping people based on their outer appearance, lack of respect for individual cultural and gender expression, racism, prejudice and discrimination have caused bullying to become one of the number one causes of teen suicide and homicide in America. We as a nation MUST take serious strides to teach and model for our children compassion and tolerance for cultural differences. We also must teach our children to stand up and unite against bullying and against bullies. If not us, who? If not now, when?

I am deeply honored to work with my colleague and friend, Azaan Kamau on yet another distinguished project by Glover Lane Press. May all who read these words be transformed…

The Letters to My Bully Editorial Staff felt that Robert LaSardo's testimonial was so powerful and profound, it needed its own stage.

Foreword by Actor Robert LaSardo

Yes. I remember my first bully. It started when I was a child. Those who looked after me were the first to introduce me to physical and emotional violence. I remember feeling a death like paralysis and a complete sense of helplessness. I was too young to fully comprehend what was happening to me or why. I just remember thinking, "she is going to kill me, my mother is going to kill me." It wasn't 'til many years later and with the help of counseling that I came to realize she was mentally ill. With the application of tools I found within psychotherapy I was able to develop an objective perception of myself independent of guilt and shame.

Years prior to treatment all I had was a collection of ideas that pointed to me as the chief culprit behind the blame. I am bad. It's all my fault. I am evil. I don't deserve to live. Monsters can be born within the minds of victims who find no refuge from the assault that comes from individuals who feel justified in tearing others to pieces. Children can be cruel to one other when there is no guidance or moral fabric placed upon them by their parents. I was nine years old when a boy my own age exclaimed rather loudly to me, "Your mother is crazy!" He was very matter of fact about it. I remember the shock of this news as if I was outside myself looking at my life as a spectator not fully comprehending the significance of his statement. Only the fear I knew. And this nagging secret hidden within my mind that I shared a space with a woman called mother who frightened me. Suddenly, what I thought had been hidden was exposed bluntly in broad daylight to an audience of children who stared at me in a way that made me feel contagious and alone. I can't say at this stage I remember being teased much by other kids. If this young boy's intention was to humiliate me his declaration served more to show me how valid my fear was. Whatever shame I carried over the realization of my circumstance, more immediate was the instinct to survive and not be crushed. It would be later and in my adult life that this shame would impact my life. In the meantime I existed in a circumstance that was unpredictable and extremely volatile.

As a child I witnessed both my parents physically attack one another in private and public for reasons I did not understand. Though I remember feeling responsible for it, I returned home from school one day to find the apartment literally turned upside down. One of the windows in the living room had been smashed. The clay potted plants had been thrown through the glass and were shattered in the court yard down below. The couch had been turned over and dishes were in pieces on the floor. The television had been knocked off its stand and vomit covered the rug. I did not know where my father was but I knew this had all the markings of my mother. The rage that came from a wounded place within her would bring storms that I could feel in my stomach. As she shook me and screamed in my face, "Your father and I are putting you away!" An endless chorus of accusations she fired at me as I sat frozen in a chair one night. I remember watching her pace back and forth ranting about things I did not understand. I remember a fear so great that I could not stop shaking and the stomach pains that seem to cut off my air supply.

These symptoms are universal for any human who has been placed in a corner tormented and beat. I share this particular life experience to point out that abuse or bullying can take any form. Let not the form deceive you. Mother. Father. Son. Husband. Wife. Daughter. Boyfriend. Girlfriend. Classmate. Priest. Rabbi. Government. Religion. God. Television. Anyone. Anything. Can manifest "the bully"

It is one thing to feel secure within a friendship and among friends who participate in some harmless joking for the sake of humor. It is quite another matter to have no friends and to be singled out, targeted and attacked. I think it is very difficult to make a clear distinction between verbal and physical abuse because of the unpredictable nature of abuse and its outcome. I see bullying as a progressive and destructive practice that ultimately leads to violence. And if there is more than one bully shouting a chorus of insults at the victim and these remarks are ignored by the victim then more extreme tactics are used to get the desired response. Bullies thrive on the attention they get from their devotees and if they fail to deliver a good show they run the risk of becoming victims themselves. This is when more extreme measures are usually taken. Throwing things at the victim, shoving the victim, spitting on the victim, damaging personal property belonging to the victim. All methods used to degrade, terrorize and instill fear. The potential flip side of this scenario can be catastrophic in cases when victims have becomes so emotionally and mentally unbalanced that they are driven to lethal measures. Suicide or literally committing mass murder as a way to cope with overwhelming fear and shame has become a growing phenomenon. We live in a socially turbulent time. A time of extremes. Random shootings in classrooms with automatic weapons are no longer isolated or limited to one particular zip code. We need to take a serious look at the little things we say and do to one another. And given our recent history reconsider the impact.

I felt Disbelief. Dread. Rage. Helplessness. There is a brief moment as you are hit by arrogance when you find it difficult to actually comprehend what is happening. A type of shock. I remember feeling disoriented and off balance. Once you are able to identify the form the attack takes and reference it to a past experience, any feelings of inadequacy you carry are dragged out into the street for all to see. I remember feeling the weight of dread so heavy it seemed to shrink me to the size of an ant. My attackers grew into giants as they fed off my fear like monsters as I waited to be crushed. When the body and mind have survived countless beatings there can be a temptation born of shame & rage that, for some, makes death seem comforting. There are those who become so sick with shame that they dream of destroying themselves. There are others who become obsessed with murderous fantasies and imagine killing their attackers. Sadly in some cases, these fantasies become all too real and lives are destroyed. Fight or flight seems to be the two doors we are faced with in this life. If there is a third door maybe it can be found in a friend who understands and is not afraid to walk through it with you. I remember feeling so isolated within my rage and completely helpless to carry out the measures needed to make my monsters disappear. It is mere luck that I was not destroyed.

There are many stories concerning bullying and what I witnessed in my youth that I could share. Some attacks were so violent and collectively orchestrated they were more like riots in which you felt helpless and could do nothing. Once a group of kids ganged up on my friend and I with such viciousness It felt like they were trying to beat us to death. The speed in which violence occurs is so fast it leaves little time to react. Words would not stop punches in mid flight. All I could do is try to fight my way out and hope my friend and I would survive the beating. It was a humiliating and frightening experience in which the only lesson I was taught was one of hate.

More significant to me than some of the bullying I endured in my teens was something I witnessed in elementary school. There was a girl in school who seemed to stand at a distance from all of the other kids. Or maybe she just stood alone. I remember she held her lunch bag close to her chest. She was talking but not to anyone directly. She was petting the brown paper bag and talking to it as if it were a pet animal. She stroked the bag and spoke baby talk to it. I remember seeing a bunch of kids stand back from her and laugh. Some stood back out of fear from seeing something they did not understand. This little girl seemed unaffected by the circus of insults that surrounded her. I watched her even try to engage with those who mocked her. I remember feeling drawn to her. There are only pieces of this girl within my memory now. But I remember we walked home from school together one day. Just her and I alone talking. I wish I could remember what she said to me as we walked. I don't know how we became friends but I knew I liked her. As we reached her home I remember her inviting me in. As I looked at her house and considered her invitation I became uneasy. She was so sweet in the way she tried to comfort me. "It's ok." I remember those two words she spoke to me, "Its ok." I could feel myself wrestling with fear as she pleaded with me to come inside.

I could feel her need for me and her frustration as I resisted. She tried her best with me and then finally gave up and went inside. I feel sad when I think about it. In retrospect I realize it marked the beginning of a series of encounters throughout my life with souls who were as lost and misfit as my own. I don't recall seeing her at school after that.

I miss her.

In some ways I was a different type of youth. I had a bunch of conventional ideas I carried around with me like a badge of honor. Looking back I realize how silly I was. Specifically my ideas about what I believed a man should be. I was greatly influenced by some of the traditional stereotypes I saw in movies that depicted a type of man that was physically imposing. It seemed to be a way to counter-balance a sense of smallness I felt in relationship to the world around me. A world that seemed predatory and armed against me in so many forms. The physical armor of big muscles seemed to be the solution as I measured strength in concrete blocks. I remember as a teenager walking down the street in New York City carrying a grudge and flexing some muscle. Weight training was the method that seemed to build a house I could be safe in. This superficial solution born of fear was only a Band-aid against the deep rooted wound that I carried. Though intimidating to some, my muscles failed to teach me the true strength that comes from within and brought challenges from others who were just as wounded and angry as me. In time I would utilize creativity as a way to come to terms with aggression and fear.

As an adult, the difference is I am more comfortable in my skin these days. There seems to be less of a need to flex. If I feel uncomfortable in a circumstance or with people's projections I find a place within myself that knows it has nothing to with me. If I don't personalize the mis-perceptions of others due to my physical appearance I am less likely to go the negative and become reactive. I cannot change others. I can only change the way I choose to engage them or not. Sometimes if I speak to people from a place of respect & kindness I can shift a potentially tense exchange into something light. I'm realizing more and more because of my extreme physical choices (Tattoos), I have a responsibility to educate and to play politician. When all else fails I take some deep breaths and keep a careful eye out for the ignorant ones.

I certainly do not feel a comfortable fit within the "social norm". I wonder these days or if ever, how healthy or natural the social norms ever were. Or are they a way to keep people in line. Who makes the rules and how do they reference their experiences in relationship to others and is it colored by their fears? I've watched the structures of traditional values come crumbling down under the weight of the hypocrisy hidden within them. I trust in the hearts of those who allow their brothers and sisters to simply be themselves regardless of what form that takes. The need to express love, art, thought and individuality is a universal right that should never be locked up in a category. I don't believe I was a/ the bully. The rage I carried for years and the way it manifested may have made people around me uncomfortable. Yet I did not make it a practice to degrade and humiliate others. That was never in my heart. Whatever brief deal I made with the devil manifested in the violence I carried out. When faced with my own conscience I failed to stand firm within my arrogance. My cause was exposed to me as nothing more than a frightened child behaving badly. The impact and legal consequences of my actions smacked me into realization quickly. I could not allow fear to turn me into a coward. I had to separate myself from the belief that the world and most people in it were out to hurt me. I had to forgive those who had bullied me rather than become one of them. It was difficult but I was running out of time and my life was hanging in the balance with the choices I was making.   I had to change my mind so that I could save my life and help others.

I realize many bullies are looking for attention. They might think bullying is a way to be popular or to get what they want. Most bullies are trying to make themselves feel more important. When they pick on someone else, it can make them feel big and powerful. Some bullies come from families where everyone is angry and shouting all the time. They may think that being angry, calling names, and pushing people around is a normal way to act. Some bullies are copying what they've seen someone else do! Bullies often pick on someone they think they can have power over. I feel compassion is the driving force behind understanding. Without true understanding there can be no real acceptance. To truly know someone requires time and effort. The work that goes into caring for others is necessary but may not be so appealing to everyone. For some it may seem easier to dismiss and label people since this requires no work. Tolerance without knowledge is counterfeit because it lacks insight. We merely put up with one other to avoid confrontation. This breeds resentment that ironically can lead to confrontation. We fail as a people if we do not put into practice what we can truly learn from engaging one another without judgment. Acceptance will not be forced but born from the realization that we are loved enough by others to risk peeling away our protective layer. I remember years ago working on a film for one of the major studios when I witnessed something disgraceful. There was a young actress rehearsing a scene that required frontal nudity. The sequence involved her running down a hallway wearing an unbuttoned top with her breast partially exposed.

I remember how some of the crew behaved like a bunch of school yard punks. Making inappropriate remarks and gestures in plain view for the actress to see. Needless to say they had no regard for her feelings nor did they display the least bit of professionalism. I didn't have to think for very long about what to do it was automatic. I told them to leave her the fuck alone. And they did. That's I how I dealt with that situation. As an actor, writer, and a presence in the media, I cannot be certain about the impact or influence I have made within the media. I can only hope that as an artist I have done good work and inspired the creative spirit within other artists and proved that anything is possible. As an actor I can only judge my career from the point of view of optimism. There is a line from the classic 40s film 'From Here To Eternity' spoken by the late and great Montgomery Clift, "When you love a thing you have to be grateful. Doesn't mean it has to love you back" Before acting I had nothing. Acting has given me a purpose in life regardless of how I am measured by it. For years It has been suggested to me by some that my efforts have been in vain. That I will fail or have failed to transcend the physical choices I have made that were part of my evolution. I cannot deny or betray who I am as an expression for the sake of the conformed ego. No doubt there will always be people who see me as threat to conventional structures. I may not be the one to completely change things. But maybe through some of my achievements I have shown what is possible to those who have been told to give up and bury their dreams.

As an actor that refuses to conform to social norms, and bullied by my peers, the media, the pulpit, family, friends, the paparazzi, my strength came from not sitting still in the face of a challenges. Doing nothing always felt worse to me than the fear of failing. Still

I have been beaten over the head for years with self doubt in spite of my conviction to fight. Throughout the course of my life I have found the suggestions of others to be crippling at times. It can be extremely disillusioning and painful when friends or loved ones take stabs at your life under the guise of constructive criticism with little regard for your passion or any real understanding of who you are. The disappointment and loneliness that follows can cast a shadow large enough to eclipse your brightest dream if you let it.

The same rebellious spirit that brought forth hundreds of tattoos would not leave me to bow before cowards. If I was to be mocked and defeated it would be on my own terms. So, I have been labeled, stereotyped, laughed at, locked up, cursed and finally thanked by those who understand this fight and appreciate my efforts. The love that comes from the gentle spirits has inspired me and kept me going.

I would like the world to know that Robert LaSardo, the author, the man and the one who takes a stand against bullying. I hope the spirit of my words can lift people out of despair who feel isolated and locked out of society because no one has taken the time to understands them.

As a man I hope the lord will continue to bless me with awareness and the strength to see beyond myself and into the hearts of others so that I may help them.

Words may move the spirit but without the will to stand up against arrogance you cannot affect change. I will always be Who I Am in a world that continues to sell me a lie about myself. I do not have to agree or tolerate this misperception. And I will help others stand up against those who feel they have the right to define what they do not know........Robert

Ifalade Ta'Shia Asanti and Azaan Kamau

INTRODUCTION

Azaan Kamau

Bullying is not a gay or LGBT issue. This book and my testimony are not about being gay, straight, or in the middle. Being bullied is about torture, humiliation, physical abuse, teasing and taunting by someone who feels less-than. Being bullied is a human issue.

I USED to be a victim….

I knew I was a weird kid. I looked nothing like my siblings, nor any girl at the church or school. The only thing that I had in common with most of my cousins was our copper complexion, our hair texture. I knew I stood out from the other people who assumed they were normal.

I was called *it*. I was even called 'diesel dyke', imagine that! I didn't even have a driver's license!

I was called all sorts of crazy things; freak, f-ing queer, bull in a china cabinet, he-she, boy, dog, red- nigger, stupid, ugly, dumb, bull dyke, dumb ass, weirdo, I was even called a faggot a few times! I think the girls were the meanest!

Now that I think about it, when I was a youth I was even bullied by my psychotic, co-dependent, and narcissistic ex-girlfriend!

 As a young person I was very depressed, sad, moody, and very anxious. I constantly avoided certain groups, school activities, and people. I always felt safe around my three best friends Rachel Moore, Tara J. Brown and Francisco Ascencio.

I was withdrawn from the things my cousins, church members or people my age loved. I loved music class, playing music and art class. I loved chorus, being on stage singing with Francisco and playing basketball with Rachel and Tara. I loved to dance. My brother Dijan and I would dance and sing for hours! Outside of those activities, I spent most of my time writing, playing music and taking pictures to make the pain go away.

Middle school or junior high would have been a complete disaster without my three best pals and my dedicated and committed teacher, coach, mentor and friend Marie Lutz. She is a living example of a teacher who stepped in when the school itself failed miserably!

So, of course my grades dropped, and academic performance became null and void. Instead of my family listening when I tried to explain what was happening, they just blamed it on me acting like a bulldagger! Go figure! I felt shame.

I always came home from school with something damaged or missing! My jacket, my gloves, my new Swatch Watch, sometimes my backpack would not make it home! I would try to hide my very obvious, yet unexplained injuries! I even had trouble sleeping for years. I never slept!

I was verbally bullied. I was socially exiled. From the first grade through the 9th grade I experienced physical bullying, things being thrown on me and spitting! I even had a Driftwood Farms Chocolate Milk bully! One day I just couldn't take it anymore, when my Driftwood Farms Chocolate Milk bully became vicious and demanded my milk, I gave it to her. I opened it and poured it all over her freshly pressed hair! Of course I got in trouble; the utterly homophobic principal suspended me for a few days. The milk bully never ever demanded my milk again. Instead she showered me daily at my locker with a verbal arsenal of ugly words and threats! My childhood was such fun, LOL!

Racially bullying hurts too! It's no fun hearing someone shout 'red-bone nigger', 'stupid nigger', 'dumb nigger', and 'he-she nigger'! The list went on and on! Just recently, I was even cyber bullied on LinkedIn!!!

Most of the people I called friend were bullied too….for years! I really hated watching them suffer! When my pals were being called 'earthquake-ass', 'coke-bottle eyes', 'rail road mouth', or 'pizza lips' it affected me too!

My beloved brother Dijan Bruttus is never far from my thoughts, or my writing. He was bullied, and bullied, and bullied. He was quite tormented by society as a whole. I couldn't stand it. I would always do something goofy to try to make him smile or laugh.

Today I am no longer a victim. I stand on faith and courage. I know for a fact that all of the people who hurt my feeling, bloodied my lip, or made me feel hopeless and helpless….they CANNOT define my destiny! Those people do not have power over me! No one has the power to determine my destiny but me!

If you are reading this introduction, TAKE BACK YOUR POWER!

No matter how horrible you think your life is, there are millions of reasons why you should keep looking for a reason to live.

Parents…step in there and mediate the conflict!

It doesn't matter if you are straight, transgendered, or somewhere on the LGBTQ spectrum. You deserve to live. Spirit, God, or whatever term you are comfortable with made you special. You have unique gifts that others do not posses. You are amazing!

If you or someone you know is being bullied, feeling hopeless, and in despair please by all means please call the **National Suicide Prevention Lifeline 1-800-273-TALK (8255).** They are there 24 hours a day waiting and more than willing to help. This toll free hotline is for our youth, those of us hitting middle age, our beloved elders, or anyone in need.

I love you, wherever you are and whoever you are!

Blessings,

Azaan

1. Jessica Knapp

I was five, wrapped up in pigtails and the innocence of wonder and curiosity. I wore a long sleeved shirt and held a giant piece of candy twisted inside a paper wrapper. The shirt was red, the sleeves were purple and the wrapper said Delight. That was me. That was me in spite of my first bully. That was me before he came and took away that delight, snuffed it like the last candle on a birthday cake. That was me each and every day I can remember before he came around the corner of the house, the yard, the doorway, with a balled up fist and a steel heart, and drove it into the center of my belly such that I would curl over, fold myself in half, and try to restore the wind he never failed to knock out of me.

He was born before me. In our family he was the little prince. He was handsomely rewarded for his sweet blond hair and piercing blue eyes. He was the only delight in their eyes. For one year, four months, and fifteen days he ruled the kingdom. He didn't ask for me, he didn't want me, but because I was there, I could serve as his jousting partner. The only problem was that he never once gave me a lance. I had no weapons. I had no fists. I did not possess the anger it must have taken to mercilessly continuously hurt another human being.

I was too busy feeling guilty about killing the dandelions so I could make a wish and catching grasshoppers and caterpillars hoping I could watch them grow wings. I was too busy imagining I could climb on the backs of the caterpillars turned butterfly and fly away from his tyranny.

I remember the powerlessness, the fear of rounding that corner and never knowing if he was lurking, never knowing if he would be there lying in wait. He was just a little boy and if he hit me too hard, all I had to do was to tell the step-king (father) and he would show up with bigger weapons. Punish him severely with the same weapons with which he would attack me.

The worst attack came in the dead of winter, when he lost his ability to stop the rage once it revealed itself. The end result was I couldn't walk and there were broken frozen slivers in my tiny, spindly legs from the broom he attacked me with. The step-king took one look at what was left of my childhood and stripped the little prince of his clothes and his dignity in the snow. He turned the frozen hose on him until his redness of embarrassment turned white with frostbitten forever skin, hair and heart while the queen and I watched from the kitchen window. The little prince didn't go after me too much more after that. When the snows melted, the queen took us from that castle never to return.

Fighting back was not something I was taught.

There were no boxing lessons or revenge video games or anyone to come to my rescue. I became my own dragon. Alcohol, smoke and mind altering shapes and colors brought me false courage. While I was scarred for life from the little bully prince, I could pretend I was safe by pretending I was not of this world. I could pretend my dreams were real and my life was just a dream.

My bully left few scars but he left tracks on my soul that became ruts and made it possible for other bullies to easily seek me out. And there were many. Only once did I see the shoe on the other foot – again another memory carved deep in my soul.

We had just moved to the new apartment. We weren't royalty anymore as we waited for the divorce from the step-king. I shared a room with the Queen and the little prince had his own little space. We wandered on our bikes to the new school. There were poles with chains missing their tetherballs. There was a baseball field but no crowd to cheer the little prince as he rode his bike around the bases. The remaining field was grass and there was a huge covered blacktop with outlines of hopscotch. You could hear the echoes off the walls of the little girls who were just playing the day before.

We were under the covered blacktop and I could sense another bike approaching. The skid of the brakes confirmed her arrival. She was a giant girl with long stringy brown hair, and a mean look that to this day I have never forgotten. She somehow had us cornered before we knew it and used her bike tire which was now standing as tall as she, as a weapon to pin the little prince to the wall. I could see the rubber tracks embedding themselves on his shirt. I could see his face turn as red as his pure white skin could bear. I could see the fear. He stood ramrod straight against that wall and didn't flinch as she continued to use her bicycle tire to bounce on and off his chest.

I was terrified. He was the meanest little boy I had ever met and other than a parent, the only one who'd laid a hand on me for the most part. Yet here he was being pounded against his will, against the wall again and again and again. When she finally let us go, he swore me to secrecy – just one more family secret. I never spoke of it again until I ran into her one more time. She was much older. I learned her name but never had to lay eyes on her except for one time.

I was with friends. We were sixteen. My friend knew quite a few magical people and I felt really special being invited to go with her. There were people who had found a special way to smuggle pot from Hawaii into the mainland in Dole Pineapple cans – right from the cannery – and we went by the house to buy one. We just wanted to smoke and drink our way out of our remaining childhoods. We were so carefree. I walked into that house with not a care in the world. I had to use the bathroom and was told it was down the hall. I walked into the wrong room. And there was that same girl – taller than ever—putting a needle in her arm. That was way too deep and dark for me to bear witness to. My heart was pounding out of my chest. All I could think of was that day at the school. I grabbed my friend and we left without getting the pineapple.

I myself have only laid my hands on one person—the one I loved the most at the time. I was beyond drunk, blacked out into an oblivious state of mind where I forgot who I was. She was in the wrong place at the wrong time of my anger that had been building from her withholdings. I loved her more than myself. I had no idea who I was, who I loved, how I loved, and why it hurt so badly when someone loved me but kept their distance because my love left claw marks. She said the wrong thing to me and I snapped. I would have killed her if it wasn't for the many people it took to separate us.

I was blinded by rage. Every punch and claw mark I left on her truly was making up for all the punches and claw marks left on me my entire lifetime. My regret, horror, guilt and pain lasted for many years. I could not imagine that I could hurt someone so greatly. While that was not the last drink I ever had, that was the first and last time I ever laid my hand on anyone.

Bullies. I wonder how they can live with themselves. I wonder how they can sleep at night, rubbing the hands that must ache from the punches they threw. I wonder how they must feel knowing they have people living in fear of them. I have spent a lifetime making sure that no one would be afraid of me. Too many performance evaluations and therapeutic offerings of my shadow self included intimidation, aggressiveness, standoffishness. That was external. The view from the inside was terrified, shy, inadequate, intimidated, scared of my own shadow.

The little prince grew up. He has a little princess of his own and there is another little one on the way. He was a step-king before that, with a very angry little prince inside. I don't know the ending of his happy little fairy tale as it is still being woven. I don't think he loses sleep over our childhood or the tracks he left on my soul. He has to live with himself.

There are still bullies lurking in my life. I am still trying to find out why. I have learned to take the high road. I don't make waves or scenes or noise. Sometimes I wish I did. I carry extra pounds on my body in places that spent years getting hit. I carry extra fear in my heart. I long ago stopped drinking my courage and often know the perfect thing to say to that next bully but it is always after the moment.

I want to see myself stand up to them. I want to hear myself scream at them. I want to beat on them the way they beat on me. I want to have them live in the fear that I spent my childhood in. I want them to feel the pain I felt when my bully would hit me so hard in the belly that I couldn't even catch my breath.

I want to just for a moment be in my bully's head and know what it feels like to look for the weak and delight in deliberately setting out after them. I only want these things for a moment. I just want to try and understand the person on the other side of those fists. I want to feel, just once, the rage of giving up all the glory for a new little attention-stealer.

If I can understand it just for a moment, then perhaps I will feel less victimized by it. If I could just conclude it was about them but not about me maybe it wouldn't hurt so much. Mean people suck – it says so on a bumper sticker I see all around town. It is the truth. I am not a 'mean people'. I will never understand what it is like to be that way.

I rescue spiders from the shower floor in the morning before I turn on the water because I know their parents are watching. I tell them it is their lucky day because I can't bear to accidently drown them if I have a chance to coax them from the floor to the bath brush to the towel rod.

I cry when our younger dogs bully, beat and tear open our older ones. I know they are following the law of the pack, to weed out the weak and the old but I can't stand to watch the meanness.

My wife and I have not raised our voices at each other in over ten years and even then we never came remotely close to raising a hand to each other. We are loving, gentle and sheer delight to each other and to our canine children.

We have no pity, understanding or love for bullies. We have loving, gentle people in our lives. Those that are not that way don't get past the front door. We have circles revolving around the 12 step world and not everyone we encounter is loving or gentle. I have been bullied in those rooms too, and taking the high road is my first reaction. It is the right thing. Others are watching, waiting to see how I will respond. The street in me that used to know how to fight in a pinch is long gone. I am all smoke, vapor, and marshmallows.

I don't have to make points with anyone. I don't have to call out the town to watch the duel. I have nothing to prove and I only care about a single watcher. This cute little girl in pigtails, wearing the little purple and red shirt with the candy on it – she is watching. She is innocent and untouched and needs to know that she is safe. She is the only one that needs to hear me say ENOUGH – THAT IS NOT OKAY – HOW DARE YOU – WHO THE HELL YOU THINK YOU ARE? – YOU HAVE NO RIGHT ....

And today, when I say enough, she hears me. She plays in wonder and delight and she returns to her backyard to catch grasshoppers and the caterpillars that have become butterflies. She isn't as hungry and she hears all the good things about herself when she surrounds herself with friends, instead of hearing all of the unspoken, most likely non-existent criticisms. She looks in the mirror and sees a beautiful, desirable woman, instead of a lonely, broken, terrified one. She takes risks, trusts her spouse, loves herself, and dances in sheer delight – even though she no longer has the T-shirt.

2. The Henderson Sisters

Note from the Editors: *Letters to My Bully Anthology* **is proud to publish original letters written by child victims of bullies. May all who read these letters understand the critical nature of bullying. Words are powerful. May we choose them wisely....**

Dear Bully,

I have Blount's Disease and walk with a limp. Instead of helping me, you wanted to make me cry. Do you remember when we were in the after school class and we had a fight? I defended myself instead of crying. You would call me names, tease me and tell the teacher lies just to make you feel good. Whenever you teased me it would usually be about my legs. You would say things like, "At least I don't have crooked legs." I would tell the teacher. But sometimes he wouldn't do anything about it. He didn't even care! Also, when you called me names it would usually be names like retarded, stupid, or death. I wouldn't like that. I was really hurt by your evil words.

So all I wanted to know was, why did you bully me? Was it because someone bullied you or you just wanted to know how it felt to bully someone? I'm not going to grow up with a complex just because you are a bully.

Tammy Wayne Henderson (age 9)

*****

Dear You Bully,

One day you hit and kicked me in my knee for no reason at all. I didn't like when you hit and kicked me. Do you remember on the third day of school? You also called me some mean names. You pulled my hair, took my book. You said you didn't like me sitting next to you. The teacher would sometimes make us partners for an assignment and you were so mean to me. You would not help me with the work. You did all these things to me on the third day of school and I had enough of you picking on me. So the next time that you hit me and kicked me on my knee, I kicked you back and pushed you down. That was the day I stopped you from bullying me.

Dorselene Henderson (age 8)

3. Tim'm west

bully

**By Tim'm T. West for Red Dirt Music Publishing © 2011
Featuring TreZure and Smut Stud**

Hook: Smut Stud

father heal this
troubled witness
bullies circle my existence
one can run the farthest distance
you can take your hate with this one

Tim'm Verse 1:

I'm just a kid on the block mindin' my business
making some good grades ain't never been a hindrance
but some say I'm soft
good grades emasculate me
they say I lack swag, reason they hate me
I speak too well, I act too white
'cuz I love the glee club, and I hate to fight
I'm a scientific misfit nerd they call sissy
academic honor roll church boy and so they diss me
pops say I need to man up, fight back
but I'm here to go to school, not for physical combat
I carry 9s in math, don't need it in my backpack
some days I wanna die, so I'm gonna get a gat
every day at school is a war zone
leave no child behind?
I say leave this child alone
been pushed to the edge of a chair with a noose
finally got that gat that one day I'm gonna use
(on a bully)

Hook

TreZure Verse 2:

I'm just a number in the system, shit I'm a pilgrim
Thrown around, too many homes with low income
I got these symptoms, they say I'm angry
Hell I'm a victim and this is what you made me
They let my foster dad beat me and rape me
Defeat me, degrade me
Send me to hell if you want Satan to raise me
Tortured daily, no family to shape me
Forget it just erase me
Bedtime stories?...kisses on the forehead?
Nah its lights out, daddy wants a li'l more head
I admit I lash out, them faggot boys yesterday they got the mash out
Pull your pants down since you like your ass out
Been bout six of 'em now by my last count
My future ain't a thang nobody gave a damn 'bout
Don't want your pity, teardrops, or your handouts
Trust me I'ma find a way for me to standout
I'm a bully, a monster, how I honor thy father
from the seeds he has planted and the demons I harbor
My actions and deeds will give you reason to bother

Hook

Tim'm Verse 3:

4 fights later
5 bloody noses
2 death threats
9th time I lost focus
1 principal visit where he said it's my fault
'cuz I wear skinny jeans and my voice kinda soft
tired of the back routes on the way home
tired of the forced loans
sick of the broken bones
tired of the prayer, father can you hear me
Even preachers say Jesus don't answer sissies
If I left this damn world
nobody would even miss me
except those that hit me,
rebuke me or diss me
Which is the biggest honor: be in Who's Who

or blow a hole in my head, which do I choose?
a victim in this cycle of bullies that's been abused
hurt kids, hurt kids and hung up, we both lose
I'm smarter, I calculate the height of the chair
leave a note, sorry moms I longer wanna be here
(bullied)

Hook to fade

Ifalade Ta'Shia Asanti and Azaan Kamau

4. Lindsay Delong

Dying to Escape

She rushes across their faces
flees their glances
she knows what's coming:
hatred, taunting, the cackling—
a whole that punches her to
the very core, to her spine,
so ominous—vicious—that
spackling them back is insufficient.

It's sickening.
No breakfast
because the fear is too much,
then praying
she can put one foot in front of the other
as the days go by,
memorizing
her shoes
'cause her head never
lifts up.

She tries to pull herself into a shell when they pass her by,
and close her ears to the grotesque singing—
oh, so many names,
or nothing at all—
here she exists
only for their jest:
they take pride in the ridicule.

Day after day
she is freshly painted
by the pain of their voices.
Nauseated,
she walks into the cafeteria, embarrassed,
ashamed,
and places herself

alone
on the bench because
no one will have
her company.

She is the
disease
on their hands,
and after she exits
the yellow bus
from another ride of torture,
in a final act
of defiance,
smashes her
glasses
to the ground.

Measurements

They saw her,
strange, livid and scraggly,
and speaking collectively of the rage,
of all she had not become to them…
their measurements—
the satisfaction
of exiled awkwardness.
Precision
was the furthest
from her understanding
but when she walked the line
some noxious mixture
of want and dread
propelled her
to stand straight-backed,
facing obscurity and apathy
choked out a voice
That the words found:
This is My creation.

Ifalade Ta'Shia Asanti and Azaan Kamau

5. Scott Taylor

Sweetness, I was only joking …

Flashback to 1985, the year my nephew was born and my grandmother died of cancer at age fifty-seven. I am now twelve years old, at the on-set of puberty and everybody in the country is talking about this new disease that gay people get called AIDS. It supposedly destroys your immune system causing swollen glands, night sweats, severe diarrhea and wasting. Images of emaciated young men in their twenties and thirties lying in hospital beds with sunken eyes and open sores all over their bodies flash across the television screen daily. They say that there is no cure for this new disease, and it is not known (at least to the general public) exactly how contagious it is.

"You can get it through kissin'," the school kids rumor, "or by breathin' the same air as somebody who has it."

"My preacher said that God made it to punish faggots for their sins," another adds, "Silly faggots. Dicks are for chicks." Laughter and chuckles abound.

"My mom won't let me go to the pool anymore because she said you might swallow some water that has AIDS in it."

"I heard you can get it from using public bathrooms."

"Well I heard that if someone with AIDS accidentally cuts his finger and the blood gets on your skin, you'll get it too."

Irrational fear had not only overtaken the country, state and small town in which I grew up, it had also penetrated the very middle school where I was attending eighth grade. Although none of us had probably ever come across anyone in our own lives who even remotely resembled the images we saw on the nightly news, we were sure that we were all at risk, and that it was probably just a matter of time before this plague made its way into our own little community. There would be "big trouble in River City," just like that musical predicted.

My own reaction to this hysteria came in the form of obsessive paranoia. I would often scan my body looking for any signs of the disease's development. Although I had never even touched a boy, an unexpected bruise, dark spot on the skin or irregular bowel movement could trigger panic. I was convinced, due to the sensationalized media and religious propaganda, that AIDS was something that naturally developed just from being gay, and that it was only a matter of time before I too would fall victim to the virus. My fear wasn't a fear of death however, but rather an irrational fear of being found out. Once the symptoms developed, everybody would know that I was a faggot. As far as I was concerned, the virus was already inside my body, given to me at birth and just waiting for an opportune time to make itself (and consequently, my true identity) known.

Eighth grade was a particularly painful time in life for many reasons. Not only did I have to contend with my irrational fears, the first significant death in my family -- that of my grandmother, and the typical ups and downs brought on by puberty, but adolescence had made the taunting and teasing that I endured daily by all the other kids even more severe. Although I was never physically attacked for being 'different', the harsh words, ridicule and social isolation that ensued tormented and pained me more than any beating could have ever done. It is not true when they say that "sticks and stones may break your bones but words can never hurt you." On the contrary, words are often much worse than kicks and punches for they have the power to scar one's soul for life. They tear at the psyche and strip you of your self-esteem. They leave tender, mental bruises in your memory and cause open wounds in your spirit that scab over and ooze misery. These psychological jabs have a wonderful knack for resurfacing at crucial moments in life (i.e. during a job interview or school entrance exam). They prevent you from making new friends or socializing with colleagues. They render you silent, crush self-confidence and consequently jeopardize chances for success and happiness.

And T.S. Eliot was so wrong! September, not April, was the cruelest month, at least for me, for it brought on the ringing of school bells that signaled another year of isolation and torment. 1985 was especially brutal. Prior to this year, I had managed to basically stay under the radar. No, I didn't really have any friends, just classmates who wanted to copy my homework. I willingly obliged, thrilled at being able to offer the "cool kids" my services. It made me feel a part of the group. Of course no one ever invited me to their house for a weekend sleepover. I attended no birthday parties or had any for myself for that matter either. Whom would I invite?! I didn't belong to any clubs and my lack of athletic ability assured me of being the last one picked for a stressfully humiliating game of basketball or volleyball or whatever instrument of torture the physical education teachers had devised for that week. But somehow I had managed to find a niche for myself in two predominately female activities—typing class and spelling bees.

I originally wanted to learn to play a musical instrument and join the school band when I was in sixth grade but my parents wouldn't buy me an instrument. I had to choose an elective so after an uninspiring attempt at an art class, I eventually enrolled in typing and enjoyed the relative isolation and useful skills that it provided. ASDF JKL I typed over and over mastering the home keys. Before long I had become the fastest typist in my school. JUJ KIK LOLP. My fingers sped along the keyboard pounding out letters and punctuation marks faster than any track star or football player could ever hope to achieve on the field. My talents would be tested in the championship of dactylographers. The coveted "Typing Bowl" in which I would emerge victorious, typing out letters at unheard of speeds with the precision of a surgeon's scalpel. By the time I got my first job as a typesetter, the summer after my senior year, I clinched the interview with a typing test of 107 words a minute! I was the man!

Of course, outside the safe confines of the typing room, I remained an open target. It wasn't that I was so overtly feminine that one might mistake me for a girl, although I did have fair pale skin, curly golden locks and cute little dimples that women adored. It was rather that my demeanor was not gruff enough for the locals. I wasn't aggressive. I didn't enjoy sexually harassing the girls, grabbing at their asses or pulling their bra straps.

I didn't play sports, wasn't interested in cars, hunting or building things by hand. I certainly didn't find flatulence, burping or other various bodily functions amusing or worth sharing with others. Instead, I was painfully shy, soft spoken, introverted and terrified of being noticed. I would go all day long without using the bathroom out of fear of running into hostile boys who might use the opportunity to clobber me. I ate lunches alone and gym class was my worst nightmare because it meant entering into the dreaded locker room – a no girl zone – and stripping down in front of my male counterparts. I remember that I would often try to skip school on gym days feigning illness, sprained ankles and wrists, headaches and stomach aches. Anything that would keep me out of that locker room, that chamber of hell and away from those demons, otherwise known as teenage boys. The lowest grades I ever made were in P.E. But that year, humiliation decided to follow me out of the gym and into the classroom.

I was in Mrs.G's Advanced Reading and English class when the nightmare began. Mrs. G was on maternity leave that year and so we had a substitute for the first semester. I suppose that, since the regular teacher wasn't there, the kids wanted to push their boundaries a bit just to see how much they could get away with. It was at this time that the teasing and ridicule stopped being a private affair, something that would take place in the locker room, on the bus, or in the hallway, and instead became a glorious form of public entertainment. I was a modern day Hester Prynne, put on display for ridicule and humiliation, but instead of a scarlet letter "A" emblazoned on my chest, I wore the tell-tale signs of fagdom -- limp wrists, a swishy walk and enough Aqua Net to keep that hole in the ozone layer expanding exponentially for at least another twenty years.

The new teacher had us seated in alphabetical order, and luckily, since my name came toward the end of the alphabet, I was placed in the far corner of the room beside T, a new girl at the school, who, due to her good looks and designer clothes, quickly rose to the top of the school's social hierarchy. I was glad about two things. First, I was happy to be tucked away in the corner, out of sight from the majority of the other students. Secondly, I was glad to be seated next to T who offered the double good fortune of being both a girl (as I felt more comfortable with girls) and a newcomer who didn't yet know of my status as the "official school fag." Of course, that would quickly change and she too would soon join the others and take pleasure in excluding poor Rudolph from the reindeer games.

The first few weeks passed relatively painlessly. I went about life in my usual fear and isolation (something to which I had become quite accustomed) and felt that the day had been a success if I managed to make it home without having been insulted or noticed by others. My grandmother was in the late stages of her rapidly growing cancer and her imminent death. That preoccupied the majority of my thoughts, so even if I had been targeted, I probably wouldn't have noticed it much as more pressing concerns were weighing on my mind. I had become aware, however, that whenever I was called upon to answer a question in class, some of the other boys would mutter under their breath the word "sweetness." At first, I didn't think anything of it. Perhaps I had misheard or perhaps they were referring to something else.

They eventually became more bold and brazen in their utterances, no longer caring to keep their remarks subtle. Now when the teacher would call on me, they would openly and brashly tease me with the new nickname they had adopted for me, "sweetness." The mocking that had started with just one or two of the boys soon grew to practically an entire classroom of students. I was no longer addressed by my first name, but came to be known by everyone in that class as "sweetness," not a very flattering nickname for a twelve year old boy. Every time I heard the word, it would sting in my ears. My face would flush red out of shame, embarrassment and anger. The teacher did or said nothing to stop them. In fact, I think I even saw her smirk a couple of times. The students had free reign.

I would often fantasize about how I might respond to their cruelty. I didn't enjoy being publicly humiliated and wanted to scare the living hell out of them, give them a little dose of the same fear that I dealt with on a daily basis. Much like the members of the "Trench Coat Mafia" at Columbine High School, I would dream of executing a quick and violent action, one that surprised and stunned -- my own little microcosmic 'shock and awe' campaign. I envisioned violently hurling my desk across the room, shattering windows and knocking over chairs as I pounced upon my tormentors, thrashing them with my fists, kicking them relentlessly in the head and stomach. I wanted to demolish the classroom, ripping up books and papers, using them to smash the pimply faces of those assholes who so enjoyed making my life miserable. I wanted them to feel the fear and pain that they had caused me, unleash all my demons on them like a pack of hungry wolves that would rip and tear them apart until there was nothing left. Only complete obliteration would suffice. Instead, I did nothing. I sat there and went further and further into myself, into my closet, filling my life with mind-numbing typing lessons. DED KIK LOL. Spelling bees, feigned illnesses and bi-weekly trips to the hospital for my grandmother's radiation and chemotherapy treatments, hoping to disappear, secretly wishing I had been born a girl so that I could have been accepted by others, acceptable to myself.

April showers bring May flowers. Winter gives birth to spring. From the dust, the dead shall rise. And so it was for me – a silver lining in my otherwise cloudy life. B made her grand entrance into my life (though if you were to ask her now, she would probably call it her grand re-entrance, as she has always been convinced that we have spent many a past-life together, as a set of spiritual twins traveling in and out of each other's destinies, through time, through the universe, through eternity, through dimensions unknown) on the first day of classes when she was shocked to see that "redneck who always wore untucked button-down shirts with the sleeves rolled up and high-tops" in her advanced Algebra and social studies classes. We had actually met each other before but only briefly and at a distance, in sixth grade when I sat next to her then best-friend, M in math class. She had presumed, as I had of her, that I was a "redneck" since that social clique was about as close as either of us had ever come to ever finding friends. B, being a sort of outcast herself due to childhood obesity, ran in the same outcast circles as I, though our paths had never really crossed in any significant way.

But alphabetical order can determine destiny and since our last names were separated by only two rather uncommon letters for last names (U and V), B and I were seated next to each other in class. The rest, one might say, is history.

Click we did. We shared so many commonalities—mutual acquaintances, mutual courses, a mutual love of swallowing bubble gum. We soon discovered that we had been born in the same hospital and only two days apart. We were both Libras. I often joked that she had seen me naked in the maternity ward. When we were older and had done way too much experimenting with hallucinogens, she decided that we had probably both overdosed on heroin in the early seventies at the height of the San Francisco counter-culture Haight-Asbury scene and had been reincarnated and transplanted 3000 miles away in a small town in Tennessee where we might recover. It had been one hell of a trip!

So suddenly, there was B ready to take center stage in my otherwise empty theatre. She seemed oblivious to the others' opinions of me and I loved her all the more for it. We existed in our own little bubble when we were together. No one else really mattered. We talked incessantly but I don't even know what about. And when we were separated by our social studies teacher and placed on opposite sides of the room for talking too much, we resorted to sign language. Nothing could stop the chatter. It was as if two old friends, who hadn't seen each other in years, were finally reconnected. There was immediate understanding and acceptance. Maybe B was right. Maybe we had been reincarnated after all.

Ifalade Ta'Shia Asanti and Azaan Kamau

6. Ed Madden

Playground

Rutherford Elementary, 1970

When Mark Nicholson spilled his milk on me—a slosh

across my lap—the teacher let me tip the rest

on him, then slipped me in some spare jeans in her closet,

and that was that. From then on, *teacher's pet.*

Carroll Toddy fell out the seat of a swing that fall,

knocked him out, left a knot on his round head

like a horn. On cold days, our teams devolved

to backwards tag, the boy with the ball running the field,

and all the rest after him—*smear the queer*—trying

to tag or tackle him. No way to win. Tagged, he'd toss

the ball, lob it in the mob of us, or hurl it high—

snag it and *you're it*—scramble past, run cross

the yard. No out of bounds, no teams, no rules,

until the bell called us back inside for school.

*His poetry has been previously published in *Assaracus.*"

Ifalade Ta'Shia Asanti and Azaan Kamau

7. Rachel Towns

Stories of My Youth Poem

We were all so cruel back then.

Angry children hiding behind a mask of perfect and innocent youth.

Blonde hair and blue eyes. You and I could have been twins except you were a pole and I was a bean bag.

I can remember you coughing in my face

Pushing me out of the way

Anything that would hurt me.

Tiny things sometimes like the scarab beetles of annoyance

But they grated like shells on my spine

Dragged me into my cocoon

Hiding in a shell of a library and

Carrying the books around as shields

I don't remember you coming to my birthday party

Although my mother reminds me of it now and then

I remember holding a toy in my hand and that it was my birthday

One day you tried to take my book

I tried to get it back

We ended up

Me

On the floor

You

Pulling out my hair

I had a bald spot for weeks

Later I wondered if you were bullied too

You were always alone as well

No friends to talk to

No library to keep you safe

Was hurting me what made you feel good?

It worries me that I might have hurt people myself

My own hurt spewing out on others

And I wouldn't have even seen it

Torn into strips and alone as I was.

8. Tom Rastrelli

Dear Bullies

I don't want tolerance. I want compassion. I don't want pity. I want action. I don't want religion. I want the Constitution.

I don't want tax breaks. I want joint federal filing status. I don't want my job search restricted to states where I have marriage equality. I want the Defense of Marriage Act repealed. I don't want to be "gay married" or "same-sex married." I want to be married.

I don't want childhood friends un-friending me on Facebook. I want friends forever. I don't want college friends calling me evil on my blog. I want collegiality. I don't want my big sister phoning me on Christmas to condemn me, once again, in the name of "Holy Mother Church." I want my mother's hugs, my dad's ravioli, and my grandma's grasshopper pie.

I want only my portion, the 1138 federal marriage rights I'm denied.

I want a wedding.

I don't want a rushed ceremony at city hall between court rulings. I don't want to wear the dress. I don't want my daddy to walk me down the aisle. I want my little sister to be my best man. I want my nieces to throw flower petals. I don't want a rainless day with perfect weather. I want a marine layer and worldwide carbon emissions reform.

I don't want to wait for the majority to feel generous, for the polls to catch up, or for the "Greatest Generation" to pass away. I want to drive the length of Wilshire Boulevard without seeing a bumper sticker that implies I'm a second class citizen.

I don't want to hear "the other side" to the "same-sex marriage" "debate." I don't want Sarah Palin, Rupert Murdock, and Rush Limbaugh.

I don't want a self-proclaimed "fierce advocate" in Washington. I want prophets who will force-feed the ground-up remains of outdated idols to their unenlightened fold.

I don't want to spend millions on political advertisements. I don't want to march in the streets protesting ballot initiatives and court decisions. I don't want "special" rights. I want people to realize that civil rights are not contentious.

I don't want fists. I want hugs. I don't want drama. I want dramaturgy. I don't want gay men playing straight roles in Hollywood. I want straight folks to live a day in my same-sex (permanently) engaged life.

I don't want to wear pink shirts every day. I want to wear them every other day. I don't want to hot-rail crystal meth while having unprotected animalistic butt sex with multiple partners at bathhouses while snorting poppers. I just want to make love to my husband. I want people to stop using my love as a weapon in their culture war.

I want to walk outside holding my fiancé's hand without listening for an increasing tempo in the footsteps behind us. I don't want to read about another gay child being bullied and committing suicide. I don't want to hear my parents crying after a stranger shouts "faggot" at me from a passing vehicle. I don't want to be hanged on a barbwire fence outside of town. I don't want to be an intercession at a church service. I don't want to return to the priesthood or the closet. I want my old seminary and priest friends to stop drinking themselves to death.

I don't want to die alone in a red state's emergency room. I want to die with my hand in my husband's. I don't want an eternity in heaven. I don't want hell. I want people to stop projecting theirs onto me. I want to make the most of the frail life I have here on earth.

I want to sit on a boulder by the Mississippi River in my Iowa hometown and rest my chin on my husband's shoulder, his warmth against my chest, as fireworks shower the nation in pastel freedom.

Ifalade Ta'Shia Asanti and Azaan Kamau

9. Jeremy Halinen

The End of Time

After church, the older boys

chased me. I was all tongue and lifted

lips, thought they wanted to wrestle

me down and kiss me.

But they took my crutches

and ran off laughing.

One returned and muscled me down.

He sat on my chest

and, before I could get a hard-on,

lifted my head toward his

and smashed it down on the sidewalk

again and again, like an innocent cock

forced to try to rape the cold, hard ass

of a statue, the way death

itself is never the end

but always the means to it.

Ifalade Ta'Shia Asanti and Azaan Kamau

10. Ona Marae

Dear Bullies of my Youth,

I sit in the park writing you, listening to the shrieks and voices of the children on the playground 100 yards away. I wonder if any of them lead the life I led. They sound happy, but I also learned to fake it. The only exception is that you stole my voice. It would take me years and years to regain it.

For a while the bullies ruled my life; your name was Legion. There were less than 175 students in my four year high school in rural Kansas but it seemed like each and everyone one of you took a turn. I know that is probably not true, but as the "fat kid", I <u>knew</u> that everyone noticed and at least of 100 of you commented on it within my hearing. In my head I can list over twenty of you who took particular delight in goading me, in seeing if you could make me break.

The worst bullies, however, were my own family. When I gave up drinking mid-freshman year, my sisters, brothers and stepmother took great delight in noticing the fact that I didn't start

Saturday with an 11 a.m. beer as they all did. "Baby, Chicken, Wussie, Wimp, Goody-two-shoes" and a plethora of other names haunted my existence in that house.

The hardest to tolerate, however, were the jokes from my own father, the man who had "loved" me enough to teach me to slam a six pack when I was thirteen. That was the magic bullet that took away my awkwardness and gave me social skills in a drug and alcohol dominated world. His disdain and sneering comments almost tore my heart in two. In fact, at the time I thought it had.

What you, the bullies who tried to terrorize my life, didn't know were two secrets.

First, the drinking that "gave me" social skills also robbed me of my wits and the ability to protect myself. At a keg party in the country, the summer after eighth grade, I was gang raped by three twenty-something men. That weight I packed on was weight to protect me, to make me unattractive to men. What you tormented me about was life saving to my traumatized mind, soul and body. I gave up drinking for the same reason—to be able to protect myself. Your taunting was a weapon, no, many weapons, against my attempts to salvage what was left of my innocence and my openness to other people. What your words did, in effect, were to seal the coffin on my fear and self hatred. They simply validated what must be true.

The other secret was an even deeper and darker one. Only a few of you guessed it and then only in joking. But those occasional hits on the target horrified me. If life was this much hell because I was fat and didn't drink, what would you do to me if you discovered I was a lesbian? It wasn't a reaction to the rapes, I had been attracted and in love with girls and women before that occurred. It was just who I was and your dissection of that would surely slay me.

So I slid further into the closet of denial and self hatred, not even from actually bullying, but from the power of the fear of bullying.

It would be twelve or so years later that a poet helped me find that voice you bound in fear. "Your silence will not protect you," said Audre Lorde: Black poet, mother, teacher, cancer survivor, lesbian, daughter of Caribbean immigrants, warrior. Her collected works grace the shelf above my writing space and that bumper sticker sits in front of them. Her poems, especially "A Litany for Survival", (from <u>The Black Unicorn</u>, 1978) gave me the courage to write my own truth, my own life and reality. She spoke for me before I could.

And so to you, my bullies of School and Family, my final word is this. <u>YOU DID NOT WIN.</u> I am a fat lesbian, (albeit a slimming one as I lose the need for protection) who loves herself and doesn't give a damn what anyone says about either state of being. I love my body and love my experience of love as a lesbian.

I am no longer trapped in the coffin of your bullying and while I do not believe good comes because of evil, I believe good comes despite evil. The good that came for me despite your evil words and deeds is that I am stronger, more vocal, more attentive and more resistant than I used to be, or than I ever guessed I would be. I am active in the anti-bullying movement in all its forms and was before that movement ever formally began. I know the death that comes from bullying and I know the life that comes in rising from the ashes of what it left behind. You did not win. I hope you found a path to happiness that does not depend on demeaning and stepping on others. If you didn't, that is sad. If you did, perhaps

you can join me in my happiness by understanding the

consequences of your actions and making things right.

11. Nova Jade

Parents Encourage Your Children: Letter to Myself

The trickle effect
The love unkept
That condition that really put a damper on our Love.
Family, the intersection of our paradigms bring up emotions that
were taught
and learned and passed on.
The love that seemed real
until it seemed bully-ish, harsh.

If I could write a letter to myself, I'd tell Me that everything you
learned
was not Truth,
and that You could stop the abuse
the Lineage of harmful, "I didn't mean to say it."
Buy yourself time, 'cuz you Did Say those things, though...

But beneath, there was Love.
The kind of love that told you to be better
even though you gave it your best.
But championships are so fun.
Trophies, we have all become.
What is success?

Is success love?

I believe is a statement that I've made mantra.
I dance to rhythms to make some more headway
into what I truly feel love means.

Is it a verbal epithet that is disguised in pure, deep love?

Is it the commands, the brash hits that pour out as soaked, drenched
Tears,
Blood,
Violent tendencies passed on out of Love.

And turn into becoming another year older,
remembering how far you've come,
weaned and groomed in That Specific Type of Love
that you learned,
That Taught you, even with the best intentions,
a botched way of displaying Support, Encouragement and Yes!

That Taught you that, would you just be better,
You'd be Recognized as doing your best
and someone would say, "I see it."

Without, "you could have done better," when the stopwatch clearly states another record was won.

Love is a pure word.
Love is a song.
Love operates not on the plane of Fear,
But on the Plane of Creativity, which subsequently, Lives on Planet Goodvibe.

My goodness, no one is perfect, but if you made the Child,
Love the Child.
Embrace their faults, correct the ones that come to harm them or Others.
But, by summit ascended, Show them that you see their effort,
so that another Child will learn to self-heal and not attempt to take their
Life

Their Love
Away from this world at 13.
Yes, even like Me.

Addendum, Message to the Youth:

It gets confusing, it gets crummy,
But, by gummit, Love it.

Love every ounce of the arghs and blahs,
Show up.
Do your best, Figure out your Bliss,
Ask. Listen.
No, really. listen.

And in between the Silence, Listen to the Voice that whispers,

"You're good. Overcome."

Ifalade Ta'Shia Asanti and Azaan Kamau

12. Jasper Odasor

You Throw Like a Girl!

The afternoon light filters through a glass of water. I wonder how something so ordinary held the power to create and destroy life. "Drowning in a glass of water," was a term used by my grandmother to describe someone consumed by an apparently "small" problem. Children are such impressionable creatures that their memories, whether remembered or not, sculpt their later years much like water to stone. Do you remember the feeling after a slur in a crowded cafeteria, a cyber-rumor gone rampant, a shove during recess or simply being ignored? Playground politics may seem trivial to adults but the same glass of water can represent a typhoon to a child victim of bullying.

My father was the tough, blue-collar epitome of hyper-machismo, in the Neolithic sense. He served as both my role model and bully. When I grew tired of emulating him and failing, I became my own person. But that took a lifetime.

In Anoka, Minnesota, the school system, largely in Michelle Bachman's congressional district, has had eight suicides in two years. At least four of the victims' families insist that homophobic bullying was behind these suicides. School officials minimize or dispute the "gay factor" as the driving force behind these deaths. The NY Times reports the victims' families complaints of a "gag order" on teaching sexual diversity in the classroom. School Officials are, reportedly, turning a blind eye to homophobic verbal/physical assaults. Nationwide, conservative voices and churches are excluding school curriculums on sexual diversity from entering American classrooms. Be anything but naïve: Why would they protect and embrace children that they would prefer to see simply disappear? To acknowledge LGBT kids exists is to accept that homosexuality is innate and not a sinful lifestyle choice. Those still living in the Dark Ages prefer the denial and suppression of these "unnatural ways." Protecting their rights would only declare their legitimacy. Many victims of homophobic bullying aren't even homosexual but are bullied for not conforming to the narrow mold defined by their gender roles. I grew up a Nerd in the Bronx where brawn and street-smarts outweighed brains. Words like "punk" were precursors to the harsher "fag", "gay" or "homo" slurs.

What lies at the root of homophobia? In its soil, breeds a hatred for the feminine. Far-fetched? Ballsy? Well, let's examine balls. When a woman has *cojones*, she's a gutsy, confident dame with *hutzpah*. Calling a man a "Pussy" won't get the same results. When adults say "Don't be such a woman!", they convey to boys "you are feminine and that's shamefully God-awful". Why would anyone *but a woman* voluntarily simulate a woman? This legitimizes bullying and teasing in boys. If you thought the only perpetrators of bullying are "tough" guys, you'd be wrong. I was bullied and teased by girls with hateful, lashing tongues. My father had hairy forearms with Vienna sausages for fingers which he used to splash on Old Spice and eat meat. The thought of associating my father with these pre-pubescent bitches brings me tears of laughter.

When females say things like "Man up!," or the title to this essay, they become both victims and perpetrators of this disguised, self-hatred-Yes, FEMALE MISOGYNISTS! Our society's internalized, unconscious hatred for the feminine, which predates the vilification of Eve in the Biblical fable, lives in our everyday vernacular. Words transcend mere dictionary definitions.

This leaves boys isolated by both genders, causing them to implode. When a man displays "feminine" qualities, we must question our universal reaction to mock or humiliate him.

Homophobia, specifically against males, IS "camouflaged misogyny". Even the bullying of gender non-conforming girls is fueled by the belief that gender roles be clearly defined. The perpetrators, usually heterosexual males, are threatened that these women may replace their role on the proverbial, testosterone totem pole. "Maleness" has evolved meagerly beyond a brutish show of competition, strength and brainlessness.

Masculinity has been so narrowly defined that men, including Marcus Bachman, cannot conform to its ideals whether, gay or straight. When boys display any sign of sensitivity, artistic ability, intellectualism or lack of athleticism, its ammunition for bullying. For boys, the message is clear: qualities known to be feminine are weak and inferior.

American TV sitcoms display maleness in its glory. You'll see a fat, goofy, intellectually deprived *schmuck* with a sensible, intelligent wife. He drinks beer, crushes the can on his head and burps louder than the fast food, drive-thru loud-speaker.

Expecting a happy ending? Go watch Casablanca! We are all victims and culprits! By the time you've finished reading, some child has had suicidal thoughts. Whether these boys live in small towns with big, Christian agendas or expansive cities with narrow-minded folks, they grow up feeling flawed. The flaw lies in a society that permits cruelty to children. America once stood for individuality, freedom and expression. I'm not so sure now.

I admire and respect my dad, but bullies made me realize that evil wasn't the horned beast drawn in Medieval texts. It wore a lace bow with curls or lived in the critical words of a Neanderthal father. It's armed with anger, ignorance and fear. It's endorsed by religion and cultural stagnation. How can you NOT grow up to believe you were broken when the first words written on the chalkboard were "ORIGINAL SIN".

Technologically speaking, we are living in the Sci-Fi flicks of yesteryears, but it's foolish to think civilization has reached its pinnacle. So much needs to be practiced in the ways of humanity, tolerance and respect of differences. But the utopias of science fiction movies are always in the future. Schools should be safe for ALL children. We can erase bullying in one generation. Let this generation be it! Draw your own conclusions, draw a crop circle! But while we do nothing, a glass of water sits calmly in the afternoon light with life-giving and destructive powers. Every child possesses the same volatile potential. Humanity's only sin is ignorance!

13. Gary Dixon

Are You Happy Now?

I HATE YOU SO MUCH RIGHT NOW

I HATE YOU SO MUCH RIGHT NOW

I HATE YOU SO MUCH RIGHT NOW

So much so

That I believed you when you said it this time

To silence you for once and give you the peace that you yourself said that I could never find,

I decided to perform the job that you yourself didn't have the balls to carry out and decided to turn out my lights forever

ARE YOU HAPPY NOW?

I think that I am

Though now…I'll never really know for sure

I believed I was the day that I looked at myself in the mirror and said "Yes…I… Am"

My confirmation I thought was the dirt being knocked off my shoulders

For I had acknowledged a truth that hadn't been found at

The bottom of that bottle

The beginning of that 5th blunt

Or whilst powdering my nose in the last stall at the dance hall

You know…That infomercial was right!!!

For a mere free ninety nine the truth had indeed begun to set me free!

The problem is that damn disclaimer…with words so small that run across the screen faster than spit can freeze in the Arctic.

Upon closer inspection it clearly states that "My Happiness based on My Truth must clearly be dismantled because it supposedly hampers….Yours!"

Hence why a leap off this bridge doesn't sound like such a bad idea tonight.

The water down below shall wrap me in its warm embrace of wetness.

Never rejecting me for wanting to be at peace

And not this Happy Shit I guess I was the only one to find out about.

It whispers sweet nothings

Silenced

To the most deafening of echoes after about 5 minutes or so

The passing cars up above none the wiser, for the calm waves have yet to reveal its newest member.

Or maybe…Just maybe

After being kicked down these stairs for the fiftieth eleventh time

 I can find out just how nice my stay at the local hospital would be for the next ten days or so

before being laid out in the ultimate resting spot.

So out with the rope

And on to the branch

That would unknowingly acquire such a rare piece of jewelry for the next few hours or so

CRYING OUT

Because it never asked to be fitted with such an ugly atrocity

You know

I am real sick and tired of you saying my name nowhere near the style and grace that my spirit has embodied.

My tongue

Finally finding disgust in the hatred you've fed me for years

See the beauty in my name

FAGGOT

I can't hear you

QUEER

A little louder please

QUEEN

Now that's the spirit

Battyman…Shit Shagger…Anti-Man…Poofter…Carpet Muncher…Bull Dagger…Lick em Lezzie…Dyke…Lesbian…Homosexual…Raymond…Tyler…Seth …Billy…Asher…

Ayeisha…And my all-time personal favorite…Gary

You hated all of us so much

No telling how many more who have come before

That we took your pain and your frustration

And against the better judgment of our light

We decided to give you the peace that you yourself said that we would never find

We performed the job that you yourself didn't have the balls to carry out

And decided to turn out our lights forever

Are you happy now?

14. Denina Taylor

Dear Uncle Thomas,

Since I was a child, you always found a way to make me feel as small as a rock wedged between the soles of a sneaker. I still find myself looking in the mirror to try and find something pretty about myself because you told me that I was pretty, pretty ugly. Yeah, I know everyone said, "That's just a joke!" However, I didn't find it so amusing. You never apologize for anything you say or do wrong, because you never feel that you are wrong. Well, I am writing you to inform you just how wrong you are!

Why do you feel like you are in control of everything? It was spiteful of you to call a family meeting to announce, "Devonne is gay, PERIOD!!! And, she always will be!!!" Did that make you proud? To be successful at having almost the entire family disown me, making my life miserable, making me hate myself, for not being able to make "the family" happy? All because of MY lifestyle! That's crazy! It's not easy going through life, knowing that I don't have any family members to call on, yet, everyone else I'm around has their family always by their side. Mama did try to warn me, though. She told me how you, your brothers, your sister, and all of your kids were jealous of her and her kids because she was the favorite daughter, and we were the favorite grandchildren. I didn't listen and I hate it. But even if I did, I don't think I would have expected for it to be this bad.

Do you remember standing at the podium, in the church, October 3, 2001? It was Mama's funeral. You said that her dying wish was for her children and her granddaughter to be taken care of. You promised her you would as long as you had breath. You lied! Right through your fucking teeth. You lied right there in the house of God! In June of 2004, I asked you to loan me six hundred dollars to pay my rent and I would pay you right back. You told me, "You and Denae can go live in a shelter for all I care!" What type of uncle says that to his niece with a child?

It's not like that wasn't chump change to you. You remember that time you asked me if I was hungry and you pulled out a wad of hundred dollar bills? You gave me one dollar and told me to get four twenty-five cent bags of chips at the store. When Grandma lived with Aunt Michelle, I overheard her saying how she wanted to change Grandma's will. She died before she could change it.

Before she died, Grandma came to live with you. Her house was vacant but you told me and Shanelle that we couldn't live there. I thought you were just selfish until I found out the true reason.

It's too bad that everyone hated me being Grandma's primary beneficiary so much that something was eventually done about it. I know all about your tricks, you selfish son of a bitch! I know that you stopped paying taxes on Grandma's house which was in the Will for me. When the house went up for auction, you bought it back for the taxes and sold it! Dirty muthafucka! Then, without notification, like you couldn't contact either of us, you threw out all of our stuff, all of my childhood memories, my high school yearbook, Denae's baby book, her pictures, her toys, all of our clothes, Shanelle's stuff, our mother's records, which are more than likely worth thousands of dollars. Then you found a way to keep us from your house.

I know it was to make Grandma think we didn't love or care about her. Because you knew that Shanelle liked to keep her hair dyed, you told her, "Don't you ever come to my house with no dye in your hair!"

My sister should have knocked your ass out but we were raised to respect our elders. You told me, "You're not welcomed at my house, period!" Oh, but we were welcomed at your house to see

Grandma's lifeless body lying there! You are a ridiculous excuse for a human being and Grandma knew it, too! She told me she was tired of you talking to her like crap. She also told me she knew I loved her no matter how hard you tried to keep me away. It's absurd--you bullied your own mother. And, I notice something about you; it's only women that you bully. That's because you're a coward and you know a man would have got in that ass! How do you live with yourself knowing that you did illegal shit to get richer than you already were? You took me and Shanelle out of Grandma's Living Will, why? So we would have to come to you whenever we want or need something? Because we were getting the house, the car, the money and the family business? You couldn't have that, could you?

I loved Grandma more than anything and there isn't enough money in the world, let alone what you have, that could replace her. Also, God doesn't like ugly and He isn't crazy about pretty. I forgive you because I am supposed to, however, I will NEVER forget how you treated me twenty-five out of my thirty years of living! I don't care how poor, homeless or how hungry I am; I will NEVER come to you for shit because I don't need you!

Like my good Aunt Betty says, "You have family and blood relatives. Family will stick by you through thick and thin but my blood relatives are just that...blood relatives!" Thank you for showing me that you have been and always will be a 'blood relative'!

Your Niece Whom You Never Cared About,

Devonne

Ifalade Ta'Shia Asanti and Azaan Kamau

15. A.H. Scott

Maybe if people stop and listen to how the other person feels, that will be a start to having a common concern for mankind….

When you're a kid, nobody listens to you. When you're an adult, everybody listens but, no one really hears you. Hearing is something that grabs your senses. And it doesn't let you go until silence takes the stage. Hearing the tone of another's voice—be it high or low pitched—impacts a listener's interpretation.

When we listen, are we really hearing? Or are we just going through the motions? You know, that nod of a bobbing head. And, even though the words are coming from our lips, the other person isn't really hearing anything we're saying. We continue to try to get our point across to them. It's like talking to a brick wall. Their eyes are open but minds are wandering over the next horizon.

In some ways, those who ignore us completely are more honest than the people who pretend to be hearing what we have to say. I guess it's life's cruel joke--two ears and multiple levels of spliced attention. To truly hear another human being is recognizing the faintest heartbeat and self-effacing chuckle of nervousness. The warmth of our smile and theirs come to the surface. Even the glint of sorrow in someone's eyes as we speak to them on a solemn memory brings it all into focus again. Doesn't take decades to hear another soul reaching out to us. It only takes seconds to stop and let our mind and soul concentrate on the issues we are being spoken to about.

Hear me. Hear you.   A.H. Scott

Ifalade Ta'Shia Asanti and Azaan Kamau

16. Yolanda Arroyo Pizarro

Raza (poem)

When I was eight years old
I was already astute
a smart worm
a perceptive cactus
who knew at that point
that during school recess
in order to prevent my classmates jokes about my hair
my skin color
mis bembas grandes
big lips
big hips
I must get into the bathroom
to hide
or to picnic there
to write novels
to talk to my imaginary friends
there were many
legion
to laugh
to recite poems
to practice what I was taught in class
to review the math test
to fancy the teacher
and imagine she was my girlfriend
to conclude my science project
to inhale the albuterol medicine
for my asthma attacks
to cough
to perform an invisible kiss
waiting for it to happen
I learned to see my world
stuck in that bathroom
of Colegio San Vicente Ferrer

spent many years making this place my den
my cave
my hideaway

I also knew
that once I sat in class
if Mrs. Guzmán mentioned the word "Africa"
while teaching Social Studies
I was supposed to wear a stoic mask
pretend it did not happen
assume an *I do not care* attitude
thereby obviate the long awaited reaction
of José Manuel or Eliseo
or anyone else who joined in the harassment
there was always the cry proclaiming funny
Yolanda, you are African!
you are so black
so ugly black
so bembetrueno
big lips thunder
big hip hurricane
while the teacher tried to scold the commotion
(silent children
show respect for others
remember that God punishes without rod and no whip)
while she tried to implement bullying policies
that have not yet been invented
by 1978

17. Rebecca Raymer

I have just recently been introduced to the concept that my abusers were my bullies and for some reason that makes me look at all of it in a different way. I don't remember what it was like to not be bullied because I don't remember what it was like to not be abused - it all started when I was a baby.

Somehow I am more disgusted and indignant about the abuse when I think of it as bullying. Being bullied is when someone makes you do something you don't want to do or feel some way that you don't want to feel, for the bully's own sadistic amusement or satisfaction. My definition of abuse is much more tangled up in my mind and not nearly as cut and dried.

But my definition of bullying describes exactly how I was abused and if my abusers were my bullies, then it all takes on a new shape. My concept of who I am has always been very muddled by the pain and betrayal and anger of being abused. But when I consider myself as a victim of bullying, it is much easier to see that I was just a little kid in the hands of someone bigger or stronger or in any other way more powerful than me, and who enjoyed hurting me.

Being bullied taught me that I was not in charge of my life, my time, my body or my mind. It was very confusing because so many of the times I was bullied, I feel like I could (and should) have done something and I didn't. I could have screamed. I could have run away. I could have fought back. I could have been smarter or angrier or stronger.

That became a wall of shame - that maybe I had not done everything I could (or imagined I could) to protect myself. That maybe I shouldn't be outraged at how others treated me because maybe it was my fault for letting it happen.

I also became a bully to people and creatures less powerful than me. I loved the idea that I could be in complete control of someone or something else, if only for a moment. It makes me very nauseous when I think about that now, about what I have done to others as a bully. It also makes me more empathetic to those who bullied me. Maybe every person who hurt me badly was first hurt badly by someone else. It helps to look at it that way, but only because it makes it easier for me to believe that maybe being a victim did not really have much to do with me at all.

It's an awkward dichotomy to be able to empathize and relate to someone who hurt me. Sometimes my empathy allows me to be less vigilant about protecting myself from the people who have hurt me. I tell myself that I since I know WHY they hurt me, I am protected from being hurt again.

I am wrong about that. I have had to see the reasons behind my own bullying and to know that regardless of what I have been through, it will never be okay for me to hurt anyone else for any reason. And no matter what my abusers and bullies have been through, it is and wasn't okay for them to hurt me for any reason. I am only helping them to hurt me when I hurt other people and when I keep going back to my abusers for more.

It's really hard to not go back for more when the people bullying me were and are people I love. My mom, my dad, my brother, my sister and people I cannot emotionally or physically be far from - my neighbors, my teachers, the other kids playing on the same street.

Being able to see how I am capable of hurting other people, of how I have actually hurt other people, has in a very difficult way made it easier for me to overcome being victimized. There are two sides to every story and I know both of them. I know the anger and the need for control - the obsessive need for control - and I know the fear and helplessness of having no control at all.

I don't want to be a part of any of it any more.

It's really hard, though. I have been raised to believe that I have no standing, no credibility, no justification for asserting myself. It has been excruciating for me to get the point of realizing that isn't true.

If I just focus on taking care of myself and seeking to help and understand other people, I can escape the cycle of pain. I still feel pain very strongly, but I don't have to add to it by feeling shameful for hurting someone else.

There is nothing more powerful than the truth and the truth is that I am not someone who deserves to be hurt. My bullies know that just as well as I do, whether they want to acknowledge it or not.

Ifalade Ta'Shia Asanti and Azaan Kamau

18. April Mae Berza

When You Used to Bully Me

Stitching time

between the two of us,

I sew memories

I once hid

inside my locker

when you used to bully me

in high school

for some petty reason

I could not fabricate

out of my mind.

Maybe,

one day,

I am to cut this fabric

off my memory

and place it in the trash bin.

The Day I Was Bullied

Mute is the day

You locked me up in silence

Piercing my very ear

With the tears

I used to bathe myself.

Inking the night

With a promise,

One day,

I would never

Be bullied again.

A Badge of Courage

It is a miracle I've become a writer.

Most of my time, I dedicate all my efforts and hours to be the best in everything even if I am not impeccable. This I believe is from my personality. I could say I have been this ever since high school. In class, I usually ranked among the top-notchers and I owe it to the fact I am a perfectionist. Phallic narcissism is my case. I know how it is for people like me. Indeed, I have to suffer from frustrations and that I must learn from it.

"What is too good to be true is to have someone like you in this lifetime…" echoing in my own mind. I resolved to find my own identity away from my perfectionist's character. *Know thyself but in knowing, try to understand there are things better left unknown.*

When I was in high school, I had hard times. I had to transfer to a public high school. I used to study in a science high school in my freshman and sophomore years. In fact, I could say I performed well in class. My health failed me. It was not a fiasco I am what I ought to be, where I ought to be.

At first, I was not welcome by my own peers. The first day in school, I wept because no one seemed to like me or to notice me at all. *I have to do something to gain new friends.* I had no seatmates. No one paid attention to a newcomer. Silence was my only companion but I hated the solemnity of the class. It was a good idea I brought myself a book. I pretended reading it. This was amusing for others to look at. I thought I would have friends, then.

I had none. I had no one but myself.

After weeks of attending classes, I befriended newcomers, those who come from different sections going to the pilot section. They became my buddies. I could have fun with them. I could be happy with them. I could be myself.

Reading has been my only existence. People see me as a reader. I have to admit I am really a bibliophile. Five books a day is the minimum number of books I could digest. It depends. Things change, it is inevitable. As I evolved as a friendly person, my own philosophies altered. I have to revise my own set of rules about my inner self. I started to feel compassion with others. It was not enough, however.

After having a fight about grades, I feared losing my new friends.

"If I am the teacher, I would willingly give the extra grade to you," I cried. That day I talked to my English teacher and asked her about it. Why she has given me a grade higher than the ceiling is not a question to ponder. She told me I deserved it. Usually, I have perfect grades from quizzes to long tests and that is because of phallic narcissism. Literature is my lifetime. This profound learning created ripples in my high school life. I could not swim a river of tears in class for my new friends never abandoned me. I found solace with their presence. It is comforting to know someone cares. Up until now, they do. And I love them for being such affectionate friends.

Strengthened by my own companions, I become firm. I tried not to notice those who bully me. I won't stoop to their level. Yes, I would not and never will.

The truth is, I had a secret supporter.

Once, I received a book, "The Red Badge of Courage" written by Stephen Crane. Fortunately, it was from my English teacher. Her faith moved mountains of fears in my heart. She encourages me to be a better writer.

A year after, I received our yearbook. There it was. My name. my picture. Under it is my goal in life – to be a writer.

Ifalade Ta'Shia Asanti and Azaan Kamau

19. R. D. Wylder

My dearest bully,

I hope you don't mind me calling you dearest, do you? I know it's typically a term of endearment, something you would no doubt see as weakness, but the passage of years has made me more capable of kindness. It's strange how my mind returns to you sometimes, wondering where you are or if you're even still alive.

I have been robbed of many memories but I can still see you quite clearly. Your abrasive swagger and blatant disregard. Some thought you were cool. The rest were simply afraid. Me? I thought I was lucky that you deigned to speak to me instead of locking me in the bathroom as you did others. I had this misguided notion that we could be friends. You had this misguided notion that I stood for everything you didn't have but wanted. So you took it and what you didn't care for you ridiculed. Smacks and shoves with the threat of even deeper violence ensured my silence. Your ever presence ensured that I was isolated and under your thumb.

I think that was the worst of it—having to endure in silence. Believing your hate filled words that no one else would understand me. That no one else would want to be around me. I already knew that I was different. You hated me even though you kept me around. I hated myself in return for my weakness...for my stupidity in supposing that there was good in you. I became withdrawn, even though there were few to withdraw from. The thought of going to school filled me with more than the usual dread and I welcomed every sneeze and every cough, hoping against hope that a full blown illness was around the corner. That was your legacy but even the weakest can take only so much.

I fought back. I finally remembered what you never took the time to see. That there was a well of anger within me too. I doubt you can recall it or do you? Academics were never quite your forte but why should they be when your little pet was ready, albeit unwillingly, to carry out any task the teachers could come up with? Except exams. That was a whole other story. Each had to stand on her own two legs but still you wanted mine to brace you. Heated whispers...warnings. I felt something stirring within me—a rage and defiance that carried strength with it. I refused to be moved, even with the promise of a beating in the horizon. I welcomed the threat of brutality, going to so far as to taunt you to 'bring it'. I'd be waiting.

I did, you know...wait. I waited and waited. Funnily enough, I wasn't scared. Truth be told, I felt a little dangerous myself. Like a slumbering lion that had been poked one too many times. I wonder if you saw something in my eyes? Something of what had been yearning to lash out at you for so long. I wonder if that's why you never showed.

It may not have been the smartest of moves on my part. It may've been stupid and reckless. But in the end, it got you to leave me alone. Perhaps it might not be true in all instances but it was in yours. You were nothing but a bully and a coward.

My anger has cooled in the intervening years. Now that I know I can stand up for myself, I am able to see things now that I couldn't see then. I can understand how your family life, with a jailed father and a mother struggling to make ends meet, could have made you bitter. I can understand how had there been anyone you could talk to like a social worker or a counselor, you might have been able to vocalize what you felt instead of turning it into something ugly.

Had there been programs that focused on skills instead of strictly academics you might have been able to vent your anger into creating instead of destroying. But you and all those like you, had none of that.

I have thought about what I would say if I saw you again. Would you even recognize me? Somehow I doubt that you would. I have changed. I am more confident now than I have ever been. I live comfortably, not wanting for anything. I have a job that—while it may not thrill me, is easily tolerated. I have loved and been loved. Would I want to rub that in your face? I am only human, cursed with the pettiness that is characteristic of our species. But I like to think I wouldn't do that.

I like to think that I would apologize to you and I can't help but smile at what I imagine to be a look of surprise on your face.

I am sorry though. I am sorry that you didn't have the opportunities I had. I am sorry that you didn't have the support I had. I am sorry that you didn't have the strength of character that I had and still have. Most of all, I am sorry that you couldn't bring yourself to rise above your circumstances and your distrust long enough to see that some of us would have been willing to help. I would have been your friend had you let me. I would have been more than just your prey.

With Love,
No longer a victim.

Ifalade Ta'Shia Asanti and Azaan Kamau

20. Aser Peleg

My Biological Desertion

Early this morning
Ayayay learned how
Daddy can leave
Before the paint even dries
How a Path Train of anger
Like a buoy's Tempura tantrums
Can be as bittersweet
As locusts that devour
A trail of Reed Royce
Mami takes pricks of
Forgoing the flash of a disposable

Marriage because there's an Angry Chair at The End of the Poker Stable
Married because it's a braid fitted for a king and his Sabado queen
Marry because why so their sun could unlearn to abandon
Hiss home now when he alone cannot stand mom dad

Dis mourning
EU'all taught mi
How can I levee
Before Cherish dries
How a spat of danger
Khan be as bittersweet
As low costs that devour
An Oregano Trail of Bodily Evedance
The Black Window exploits
Forgoing the Flash Moab of till debt

Dew US part.

Ifalade Ta'Shia Asanti and Azaan Kamau

21. Kevin McLellan

i didn't have answers

i covered a sheet of paper

with *why, why, why, why, why…*

the monotonous testimony

of daily teenage confusion

until you took it and didn't

give it back—the evidence,

my evidence no longer mine,

i knew that you knew that i

was vulnerable, and then further

i was on the periphery… of i

I know where to walk

We stand back-to-back and face

in opposite directions (on

the speculative to non-speculative

spectrum) like before a stand -off.

There are facts somewhere

(which can, and often do, include

the unknown) and your speculation

(concerning familial matters or

furthermore human) thus upping

the family stakes by publicizing

them explicitly (your attempt

to take ownership) and I refuse to

further entangle, so I must find

the strength to continue without.

Ifalade Ta'Shia Asanti and Azaan Kamau

22. Shannon Pacaoan

For R.A.P. & V.L.P.

Looking at the fresh wound on my wrist, the world slowed to a halt. Sound escaped, and I was left abandoned in a vacuum.

I watched the blood retract from the center of it -- where the stick made contact -- scraping away the skin and the bone beneath exposed white. Once blood filled the wound and the sting began to echo from a light breeze, I snapped back to reality, aware again of my surroundings.

Cradling my wrist to my chest, I crouched low behind a shrub at the lip of a ditch for shelter. Without it, I would have been left vulnerable in the center of the abandoned field. I leaned against the sloped wall of the make-shift trench my brother and I dug weeks before. And I let the sand spill into the collar of my t-shirt and trickle down my back.

I heard the neighborhood boys laugh from across the field before they threw another stick at me, this time landing short, kicking sand in my face.

Sticks and stones. Sticks and stones.

I began to whisper the popular rhyme to myself. But sitting in my fear, I could only concentrate on the first three words. They became my mantra. Over and over again, I repeated them. I offered them up like a prayer, hoping for someone to come to my aid, some divine intervention.

This wasn't the first time I was cornered by these two boys. Nor was it the last. But I do remember it escalated from a seemingly innocent basketball game.

These same boys challenged my brother and I to a half-court game, making it clear they would dominate us because they had two boys on their team. I didn't care. I was excited! It was one of the first times my brother invited me to play ball with him. Before this, it was just drills, running lines on our driveway for missing a lay-up. And after months of training, he thought I was ready for a scrimmage. So I laced up my pink Reebok sneakers and was eager to go.

Early in the game, I had the ball. I was guarded aggressively, floating near the 3-point line. I took my time, looking at my options, plotting my plan. Could I drive to the basket? Should I pass it to my brother? But he couldn't shake the boy guarding him.

All of a sudden, the boy on me relaxed. He took one step back with his hands behind his back. He offered me a free shot. I waited for him to say, *Shoot it now!*

And I did. I listened. I trusted him. And before the ball could leave my fingertips, it was immediately blocked. The ball ricocheted off my finger, jamming it, and grazing the side of my face.

My finger throbbed. My face stung. But the humiliation was worse and I cried from the shock of it all.

I slightly remember the face of the boy guarding me twisting into laughter before my brother grabbed the sleeve of my shirt and yanked me off to the side. It's his, red-faced and angry, that I remember most clearly.

Curt, he questioned me.

Who's on your team?

Right! So, why are you listening to him? Know who to trust.

I'm not too sure what happened after. I'm not sure if we won that game or if there was an ego match that escalated into a fist fight or if my grandmother called my brother and I inside for dinner.

But I learned one of the most important lessons about living and surviving in this world through that game and my brother's words: *focus on achieving your goals; know who's on your team; and learn to listen, trust and nurture those.*

Ifalade Ta'Shia Asanti and Azaan Kamau

23. Tammy L. R. Young

You Bully!

You teased, chased, kicked me in the face, you cussed and fussed, always about my butt! You socked me, clocked me, till one day you got me. Caught me off guard, my feelings were hurt. I took it hard. This was after gym class. You laughed at me for having as you put it a "Woman's body", at the age of 12 ½ years old. You teased, poked and bruised, then accused me of things with men and boys.

You yelled I had become their joy….their little toy.

Always giving me cold stares as I walked up the hall and down the stairs. Everywhere I turned, it was more than just concern. I was scared even self-conscious going to music class. You taunted and laughed, purposely sitting by me making jokes about my ass.

You, my bully were the one that started my insecurities about my body.
Currently in my forties, but still when people say anything to me, whether it was a compliment or some negative bullshit, comments about my curvaceous body or my ass is still taboo to me.
You, were the one I thought about. Your jokes, taunts, slurs, and ugly words.

As of today, while I model this lingerie, proudly with my big ass …. I stomp the runway!

Ifalade Ta'Shia Asanti and Azaan Kamau

24. Amy LaCoe

To My Inner Bully

To be transgendered is to offend a male code of ethics as old as patriarchy. So strong is Mother Nature that She, and women, must be conquered, subdued, and ruled over by male dominion. Transphobia grows out of the same mistrust and fear of feminine power, as does Misogyny. Many but not all males, consider it their duty to defend manhood against the likes of anyone who threatens the gender binary.

I was born in 1946 and raised in the 1950's when the words transgender and transsexual didn't yet exist, so I was never bullied for being transsexual. Instead I was a sissy, mamas-boy, queer, fairy, fag, homo. I wasn't ever quite sure why I was considered those things, and heard the words before I could even imagine what they meant. I knew I felt more like a girl than a boy. I didn't know why but I knew both from my parents and my peers who bullied me that I was just plain wrong to feel that way.

Early adolescence is that time and place in a boy's life when their place in the male hierarchy gets established on the playground. If you were an easy target, there was a moral excuse for picking on you because to be weak or unmanly was also to be sissy and queer. In other words, you were deserving of what you had coming. In the seventh and eighth grade, I seemed to be the first "go to" kid for anyone wanting to pick a fight and start working their way up to more "bad ass" positions of male dominion. I was fair game, a free win under the belt of anyone wanting to move up the ladder.

Like any good parents would in the 50's, when I lost fights, got my lunch money taken, or my PB&J sandwiches stepped on. The solution was: learn how to fight back and they'll stop picking on you. My mom even told me that if I lost another fight, I'd have a spanking waiting for me afterwards. My uncle, her younger brother, had just gotten out of Marine Corps boot camp during the time I was being bullied. She told him, "Take my kid out into the back yard and teach him how to fight before somebody kills him."

After he had tired of trying to get me to stop just blocking punches and hit back, he pulled my face into one of his sweaty arm-pits and told me to stop being such a sissy and fight back. When I kicked, hit, and bit him, he praised me for it and said, "That's it. It you hurt those little bastards but good, they'll leave you alone." He was right. I survived the 7th and 8th grade. Oddly enough, kids stopped calling me sissy, fairy and fag and stopped picking fights with me.

There was no support for my inward feeling that I wasn't a boy at all. I knew before I started kindergarten that I was inexplicably a girl child. My adolescent experiences convinced me that it was simply not a feeling I could ever publicly admit to having. By my junior year of high school, my social standings had advanced from total panty-waste to likable nerd. I had stiffened my walk, taken the lilt out of my voice and reduced it to a monotone. In other words, I conformed to the male code of ethics that kept the girls and boys on the appropriate side of an enforced gender binary I always had trouble feeling.

One incident in the middle of my sophomore year could have been devastating for me, and to this day, I don't know how I escaped from it. Christmas vacation had come around. Since I had two weeks off of school, I thought I could shave my legs and get away with it. It was a crazy idea that the hair would grow back in two weeks and crazier still when I shaved them again the following Wednesday to get what I had missed the first time. A week and a half later I was back at school and had to suit up for gym class. I waited two days to suit up, but after the second day, couldn't risk the note home or the failing grade. My legs were still very bare when I did suit up. Someone in the locker room noticed and gave me a cat whistle. He got up on the bench between the lockers, strutted up to me, stuck his penis up in my face and said, "Here, suck on this! Fag!"

An older student told him to get down and stop it. He did when the other student moved towards him in a threatening way. The older student did look down at my legs but didn't say anything. If it got around the school, it didn't get back to me and I never heard more about it or had to explain it.

My experience after the eighth grade was, and is, that most men aren't malicious. At least one young man stuck up for me and probably didn't like bullies any more than I did. There is still a part of me, call it my inner bully, or my internalized trans-phobia, that holds fear, anger, and resentment over my middle school years. Even though the actual people who bullied me in middle school have no reason to even think about me today, they still populate my mental landscape. When events happen, such as the murder of a trans woman or the shooting of another just two days before the International Transgender Day of Remembrance, they also bring up a certain reality.

It reminds me that some of us are still beaten and even murdered for being who we are. Many more are still being evicted from their homes and living on the streets for being transgender. The murder of Larry King in Oxnard, California was a double tragedy because the adolescent boy who killed him learned his hatred at home from his parents, heard it preached from the pulpit by clergy and saw it overlooked in classrooms and locker rooms.

I accept that there is still hatred, sexism, homophobia and trans-phobia in the world without condoning it. I do it by letting go of my mistrust and anger lurking in the darker reaches of my mind. My fear and mistrust is of the same substance as the anger and fear that is still discriminating against and killing transsexuals today. What I would say to the kids who bullied me is that I know that some of you grew, matured, maybe even have gay, lesbian, bi, or transgender brothers, sisters, children or grandchildren. The world of the 1950's and 60's where my inner bully took shape is not the same world I am living in today.

We live in a world that is beginning to understand us and in which we can better understand ourselves. I can see the promised land, even if I am not there yet. A transsexual child born today in an understanding family has a real possibility of being heard and believed when she tells her parents she is a girl, even though she was mislabeled as a boy after a quick glance at her genitalia. The odds are at least significant that transsexual children can grow up to be loved and self respecting men or women of the gender they know themselves to be. So I say to my inner bully, you are only my own fear and anger. I say to those adult people who were bullies when I was growing up, let us all be the forgiveness, understanding and hope for a world in which all children are loved and accepted for who and what they are regardless of race, religion, national origin, sexuality or gender identity.

25. Tina Cates

Screaming Whispers…

A girl out of breath, panting, exhausted

Vulnerable to that cry within.

Screaming loudly out of jealousy and insecurities.

Not aware that she was being manipulated by that demon that laid dormant inside of her.

Fits of rage escapes her broken heart, striking blows at her lover who only knew abuse anyways.

See her woman grew up with a mother that knocked her head off on a daily….

"So this is how you show me you love me. You Love Me don't you?!"

"I DO… love you"

My soul open wide, being everything but nothing at the same time.

The bully was in my mind as the rage took control.

No longer the gentle lover I knew before. Transformed me into an unknown I dare not know.

Controlled by my emotions, unable to even see as before.

PRAYING to GOD please! "What if she says this or that, call me a bitch, call me fat…   You Fat Bitch!!!..

Ouch!!

It called out loudly, striking bones and marrow to the core.

Bloody rivers of my puddles from words said by my lover.

More lashes from lips that once tasted like sweet dripping honey dew melon,

now salty with hatred and venom.

Blow by blow it seems to never end. Rage escapes!

My shoe thrown from the other side of the room crashes into the cocktail table,

mind shouts "WHY can't we ever keep shit!!"

Terror, as if in slow motion.

Clock ticking

When will this end?

Fast forward to the next day,

finding her in kitchen wearing an apron cooking eggs???

What is this Mess!!!

Me waking up ashamed, exhausted and hurt.

Actually seeing her the victim thinking, Maybe this thing can work? More prayers,

More good days with her.

The lay down real good, the stand up unnatural bullshit...

but I never quit.

Still more growing to do.

The last encounter of the ugly kind was just an alibi for her to hit the streets.

Instead hitting the floor and a new introduction to the 4 B's:

bitter words, blows, busted lips, and bruises.

Silently whispering, It has to stop, love doesn't feel like this!!

Only seeing bits and pieces of how abusive it really is.

A day away where lessons are learned.

Contemplation, reflection, the truth un scorned.

Picked up the one thing that I learned….

The end of this would only wind up in Prison, Hospital, or the Morgue.

Screaming whispers of words that changed my life,

still knowing that HE's not done with my life.

Whispering

"You are only in control of your Response! You are only in control of YOUR Response! You are ONLY IN CONTROL OF YOUR RESPONSE!!'

I got it!

Tested in the worst way when one long night she was ready to fight.

Started the lashes, the fat asses, the whole act so I would give in like I used to.

Trying to scurry up hatred and anger, she was downright evil.

"Not this time"... Peace began to enter me traveling through my bones... "Not this time!"... Serenity circulated through my blood & touched each limb.... "Not this time!!!"...

"HE shelters me with HIS blood!!"

This time My bully won't win.

Looking at her closely, this person I loved was unfamiliar.

As if looking at her through a glass, I felt no longer imprisoned.

More words thrown but they didn't hurt anymore.

My bully didn't win, as her own rage grew stronger within.

Wanting me to turn into something I was not....

And I'm Not,

and will never be again!

Hearing old folks saying, "Baby, Bullies aren't born they're made!"

The terror that once made itself a friend to strike back was intact.

No longer living in fear of the verbal abuse that made me snap!

Made new decisions on what I expected.

One of my very first rules

No kind of Crazy will EVER be accepted.

Screaming Whispers...

26. Neil Ellis Orts

The Adults Around

Bullying has been weighing on my mind quite a lot. Teenagers are killing themselves because of it. The current focus of the media has been teens who are gay or are perceived to be gay (which makes it especially personal for me), but everyone knows there are a number of reasons bullies choose their targets. Weight, academic achievement, religion, economic status, fashion choices . . . these are just the ones that come to mind at the moment.

As a nerdy, fat, goody-two-shoes, sissy boy growing up rural Texas, you might assume I was a target of some bullying. The potential was certainly there, but when I read of what some kids are enduring (or not) these days, I cannot say I was seriously bullied. What I endured might be better categorized as being "picked on" now and then, but I was never the victim of physical violence and the verbal abuse was comparatively mild. No one ever told me I should go hang myself.

When I think back on why getting picked on never escalated to anything more serious, I can come up with only one answer: the adults in my life. The teachers at school, the adults at church, my parents and extended family—they didn't put up with the meanness that lies behind bullying. My memory may be playing tricks on me, but I do not recall anyone really being bullied in my schools as I grew up. There were popular kids and unpopular kids, but not blatant abuse. It was a relatively safe place to grow up.

What breaks my heart most of all about the recent suicides is that these teenagers felt as if there were absolutely no adults they could turn to for protection. This is inconceivable to me. Had things gotten out of hand for me, there were any number of adults who I could have turned to for help. How do these teens not feel the same?

I have no children and only limited interaction with children. Since these recent news stories, however, I find myself paying more attention to the few kids I do see daily, whether at church or in a store or on the bus. I find myself listening to their language, how they treat one another as well as how they're treated. Kids should feel like there are adults around them who care and will protect them. If I ever hear something that is outright threatening, I pray that I have the courage to say something and the wisdom to say the right thing.

I ask that you, too, pay attention to the children and teens around you and step in if things are getting out of hand.

There is the YouTube video series from adults who were bullied as kids, telling kids that "It Gets Better." These are messages of hope and I applaud them. I also believe that kids shouldn't have to wait for it to get better. My encouragement for all adults is that we make it better. If a nerdy, fat, goody-two-shoes, sissy boy growing up in rural Texas can have a safe childhood thanks to the adults around him, surely every child can have one, too. The key to that sentence, however, is "the adults around."

Let's be the adults around.

27. Jacquelyn Kennedy

Dear "*I don't know why you keep bringing that up?*",

You showed me that in our house, abuse and discipline meant the same thing. You snatched that long, brown extension cord and designed my body with big, red, tear-shaped welts from the way you curled and doubled that cord in your hand. And then you dared me to tell somebody! Your voice….I can still hear your voice pounding in my head decades later, "*And ya bet not tell nobody!*" So, I guess it was my fault that Mr. Friend-of-the-family sat me on his lap and put his hand up my dress. You did not discipline me the right way! So now it's a challenge with my own sons to lay out consequences. You taught me that my brothers, the only three male figures I loved and looked up to like role models, like father figures, like protectors, like my everything; that trusting them was a lie.

You made me believe that it was natural to be put in separate rooms from my brothers every time you left the house. Oh, you left food in there for us, but we were locked in there so long that we trained ourselves to pee in cups. That's a shame. You made me believe that my brothers would try to hurt me or abuse me sexually. I remember your voice oh so well "*and ya bet not tell nobody*!" You taught me that I "*bet not trust no man*" …so I went through life feeling empty, not letting down my walls to accept the love and kindness God sent my way. You locked me up in that box for years. I left my emotions and my thoughts there….. in that box.

Many years have passed and I really want you to know that I forgive you. Why? Because now, as an adult, I understand that you were broken and that all this happened to you too…only worse. I'm not saying you did right. I'm saying, "I understand you were broken". Time does *not* heal all wounds. It only heals them if you *choose* for it to. I chose to turn what I went through into inner strength. You chose for it to eat you up and took it out on us. But now I know…you didn't know any better. I chose for the cycle to end with me.

It is important for you to know that as many bad days as we had, I remember even *more* of the good days. You taught me how to be a creative, well-rounded, confident, educated, independent, sensible, powerful, black woman. I love you for this and thank you for this. Thank you for evolving into a supportive, kind-hearted, open minded, affectionate, joyous mother. You have always been my biggest cheerleader.

I thank God for creating a forgiving, caring, loving, and precious soul in me. Thank you, God for showing me the way to express my feelings and have a voice. Thank you, God for healing us both enough that we are now able to create a loving, supportive bond. Thank you, God for letting me have my Mom for all these years. Thank you, God for working miracles through me that I now am the one protecting, teaching, and healing her and many others. Now I know what it feels like to have a shine and a glow; my own village of loving souls surrounding me and now, "This little light of mine, I'm gonna let it SHINE!" Thank you, God for rescuing me young enough to share my life, my story, my glory, and my love to the world.

Blessings,

The One Who Still Has Your Back

28. Katrina

1984. Coconut Grove, Florida. Coconut Grove Elementary School.

Dear tormentors,

You made my elementary years miserable and that is why I still remember your names, over thirty years later. I was affected, changed, and emotionally scarred by your incessant taunts, your relentless nasty verbal attacks and your physical threats. I can recall every single detail as if it happened yesterday, in exquisite detail. As a woman if I were to encounter you in the street I am capable of cutting you down with a mere look and carefully orchestrated words designed to cut you to your core. Because I know what would hurt you to your core. Because now, as a grown woman, I have become everything you have not.

When I was a child I did not have any way of knowing the future. Of knowing that I would end up in a better position in life, with better education, with a better spiritual perspective, with better life choices. So, let's take a little journey back to the mind of that little girl that was me. I am chubby, painfully shy and with bad hair. I was different to you. Why? Because instead of worrying about what kid I was going to beat up next week, or the latest fashion, or who I was going to make out with…..I was interested in music, art, drama, and writing. You couldn't tolerate my "differentness". You thought my family was "rich" because we lived in a house, and not the projects. Because my grandparents drove a Cadillac, because I wore clean, clothes and spoke well. You loved to tell me "You talk like a white girl." Why? Because I spoke English the way it was supposed to be spoken. "You just wanna be white." you would say, as you stood there in your tee shirt with a blonde, blue-eyed Jesus on it, popping your gum, patting the itchy weave on your head and starring at me with your green contact lenses. "Why you talk like that?" You persisted. When I asked you if you knew how to speak

Swahili, or any other African language, you became silent. Point made. We're both speaking a language forced upon our people, only I'm at least speaking it properly.

You hated my intellect. You hated the future you saw lurking in my eyes. You knew I would end up being SOMBODY. You knew I already was somebody. You didn't know how to process all of my complex and simple ways. You took my extreme shyness for being stuck up, which I wasn't. I desperately wanted friends, and did have a couple. But for the most part, they all joined in with you to torture me.

On the physical education field. No one ever picked me to be on their team. I was always chosen last. Do you know what that does to a child? To ALWAYS be chosen last? To feel like no one wants anything to do with you? To think that you're an un-wanted thing?

On the school bus. I sat, clutching my book bag, praying that the wicked glint in your eye would not be turned to me on that day. That you wouldn't be in the mood to pick at me, to call me out, to push me, to have others join in your chorus of mean-spirited taunts. I prayed I would not hear the whispers saying "Let's get her today."

In the class room. Because I liked to sit near the front, because I ENJOYED learning, because the teacher liked me. Because I was an easy target, with my hair sticking up in all the wrong places. Because my grandparents made me wear clothes that covered my body instead of expose it at such a young age. Because at 13 yrs old I still hadn't kissed or gone all the way with a boy. Because I was not one of your pre-teen mom friends. Because I didn't experiment with drugs. Because I was so completely different from you and you were afraid of what was not exactly like you.

After school. I remember you, Anthony. I remember it like it just happened. I was walking home from school when I noticed you behind me. You had that familiar sneer on your face that I dreaded.

I tried to pick up my pace but you would only speed up behind me. I walked in silence, tears welling up in my yes, wondering why you wanted to follow me. I felt something hit my back. It was a rock. To my horror, you kept picking up rocks along the way and throwing them at me. I walked faster, praying you would go away, tears now streaming down my face, sweating, my heart pounding. You were laughing and throwing the rocks at me until I got closer to my house. Then you went away. The rocks felt like bullets hitting my very soul.

Fast forward several years. I am now in my early twenties. I'm doing very well for myself. I remember one day I had to go to the doctor office for a check up on my way to some other event, in which I had to dress up for. I pulled up in my car, which was a beautiful Jaguar xj6 at the time. I noticed a woman staring hard at me. She looked broken down, with four kids trailing behind her, holes in her clothing, her hair disheveled. She could not take her eyes off me. I started to feel uncomfortable until slowly her face registered in my mind. She was one of the girls who bullied me. One of the ones who made fun of me because of the way I dressed, because I didn't have a boyfriend, because I was so quiet.

"Katrina?" She asked, almost in disbelief, as she looked me up and down. I did happen to look really great that day. Unbeknownst to her, I was also doing a little plus size modeling as well. Me, the little, funny looking, fat girl was now a model. Imagine that!

"Yes. Is that you?"

She confirmed that it indeed was her. She laughed nervously as she tried to make small talk. But I wasn't interested. She asked me if the Jaguar was my car. I nodded and walked away, leaving her with her jaw on the ground.

Confirmation that everything my grandparents, my teachers and true friends ever told me. They would tell me not to feel bad, because one day I would surpass all of my bullies, that I was special but not in a bad way. They would assure me to be patient, and one day everything that I am would pay off. I didn't believe them at the time. Now I wholeheartedly do. Now I am grateful for being different, for if it would not be because of my uniqueness, if I would've conformed to be just like everybody else, I would never be the woman I am today. And for that, my bullies, I thank you. Each and every one of you.

Katrina

29. Jazar F. Kahr

As a kid growing up in a small town I was picked on a lot because of how I looked, the clothes I wore and the fact that I was smart. As I got older it became worse. I was tripped, punched, kicked and even choked. My bully broke into my house to beat me up, spit on me and just took every opportunity to just humiliate me. The teachers knew but did nothing. My mother's solution was to fight back but I was too afraid and embarrassed to do anything.

I eventually stopped even saying anything and started finding ways to avoid my bully. I would eat my lunch in the nurses office or near a teacher, I stayed to myself and always left earlier but I didn't always stay clear of my bully. I eventually got to a point of dreading school just because I knew how my day would turn out... Sometimes I wished I was dead or would just disappear. I made it thru my bullying years alone and tortured thinking no one cared. I dropped out of school early just to avoid getting beat up which caused me to go down a very hard road. Ten years later I saw my bully strung out with two kids and no job. She was so high at the time she didn't even know who I was. My anger instantly disappeared and turned into pity for her. I no longer felt threatened by her but felt sadness for her.

I remembered her mother was that way and a lot of bad stuff happened to her because she had no one to protect her. I understood why she picked on me and beat me up. Someone was treating her the same way she treated me. Don't get me wrong, it was no excuse for the torture she put me through some of which I care not to speak about even to this day but I understood. When I got home that night I said a prayer for her and her kids. I forgave my bully for hating me and forgave myself for hating her.

I couldn't help but wonder if one adult that knew I was being bullied would have stepped in and intervened or at least tried to help, if me and my bullies lives would've been different. As adults we think children are just doing a little teasing. But when a child is being publicly embarrassed and abused and no adult steps in, the repercussions could be, and are a lot of times ARE, deadly. Adults must do their part to STOP BULLYING!!!!

30. Bill Klemm

Dear Bully,

Usually my mornings consist of a frenzy of preparation and paper cutting. I need to be ready to greet those toothless seven year olds who call me , "Maestro". Mornings are usually the calmest part of my day.

Today you decided to change things. I arrived at my classroom trailer just as the morning sun was peeking through the clouds. You left a message for me on my door. Your hate greeted me. With a knife or some sharp object you scrawled deeply into my door. Over the course of twenty years I have had rude messages left for me before. But none like this.

You carved, "GAY PIG" into the door for all to see. I would guess you are the same hater who painted "FAG" on my steps earlier in the year or perhaps you are the one who leaves unwrapped condoms on my door knob? You have been busy hating me.

I don't know who you are and I do not want to.

This latest offense like the others will be painted over with school issued orange paint. It matches nothing and only serves as a reminder of what is underneath. A patchwork of hate.

I opened my classroom door and sat down on the floor and quietly wept. You won this time, this moment.

When I got up and called the office and told the clerk what had happened, she audibly gasped and rang the bells two times, signaling the janitor. He would get the paint.

I could see my students lining up on the playground. All smiles and crisp blue uniforms. In a moment they would squeeze by the janitor as he painted the door. A few would look knowingly at me. They knew I was upset. As they piled into the room the morning commotion began. Who has their homework? Who is going on the field trip?

I hope you are proud of yourself. You wounded me. You provided the first lesson of the day.

Time for the reading lesson to begin.

"Open your books to page 41 please and let's begin."

Maestro

30. Rab Marlow

DEAR BULLY

Here's a question for you: what is it that defines us as human beings? Is it how we look, act? What we say, think? What we believe in, value?

And who does the defining anyway? We ourselves? Are we whoever and whatever we say we are? (I can't altogether think so. When I was a child, I declared I was a kitten and when I grew up I was going to be a cat. This pronouncement no more made me feline than did my fervent belief I was heterosexual make for a happy marriage to a woman.)

Why then, do others get to define us? They try, certainly. Every social group sets rules and expectations for its members' behavior—and consequences for failure to measure up. Yet to be human is to be a walking set of contradictions and mystery. We each have a hard enough time getting a handle on who we are as individuals. How can we pretend to define who and what another person is? But others do hold the power to define us, don't they— in the end, we become whatever memories they carry of us after we're dead and gone.

So I ask you, Kurt, how are we defined as human beings? I was 14 when you started in on me. "Jeezo," you labeled me. "Fag," "pud," "queer." I didn't know what those words meant. I didn't want to know. I knew you didn't intend them kindly. Whatever they meant, they didn't jive with my Sunday School award for perfect attendance. Didn't jive with how I wanted to define myself: good church boy, obedient Christian, godly teen.

I prayed for you, of course. Prayed you'd go directly to hell. Prayed your arm would snap next time you pressed me against the wall, next time you thrust your hand under my chin, pushed my head back so I could see only the ceiling, had to look heavenward from whence came no help.

Every school day you tormented me. I can still feel the jibes of your tagalong henchmen, hear the snickers of my classmates. I often felt helpless, hapless, humiliated at your hands.

I wonder which affected my sense of self more, your actions or my inaction. To what extent did I participate in my own abuse by allowing you to treat me as you did? Was I so helpless as I imagined? Under your tutelage, I came to see myself as a spineless loser, stupid sap, human push-around. What recourse did I have? Over and again I appealed to God without effect. I tried to tell my parents what was going on. How to explain, "Mom, Dad, your oldest son is the laughingstock of the school, the scum at the bottom of the barrel"?

I let myself be defined by your words and actions. What about you? I suspect you were defined in part by how you looked. You were the one dark face in a sea of lily-white. How was that for you? I never asked.

Were you unleashing on me pent-up anger you couldn't blast at your friends? You had friends, right? You lettered in golf—didn't that put you in the rich kids' club? Maybe not. Maybe doors were closed to you; maybe in a thousand prickly ways you were told you didn't belong. Was that it? Or were you lashing out at something in me you didn't like in yourself?

I'll never know. You pedaling your bicycle, a couple years after graduation. A sudden roar. You never stood a chance against that Mack truck.

All that's left of you now are memories. Those, and the way I still shudder to think of you, the sour taste that rises in my mouth when I do. Some legacy, eh? I'm left to define you, Kurt, to shape you—not in the way you shaped me, but still. I wish I felt more kind.

31. Cheryl Lewis Beverly

My Bully is Called Racism

Letter to My Bully

I suggest that as we are now so appalled at the consequence of the

"BULLYING"

 of young and often gay children in schools that we also begin to acknowledge that the Black community has always been the victim of bullying/bullies in the form of racial verbal and physical attacks. **WE** had/have been made afraid to go to . . . almost everywhere, for fear of harm. Henry Louis Gates Jr. was **bullied** in his own home.

America has been our bully.

What comes to mind as my greatest confrontation with a bully is that in my lifetime because of **racism** we, Colored, Negro, Afro-American Black, African American people, were **physically** separated, by law, custom and practice. We were physically "segregated" from other religious groups and ethnicities. i.e., white, Chinese, Jewish, Polish, Irish, etc., in Chicago. We lived in different neighborhoods **with the threat of harm** if we crossed "the line." We attended different schools **with the threat of harm** if we crossed "the line." We only passed each other while shopping in the downtown area, going to the amusement park or museums and when working, and did so cautiously **with the threat of harm** if we crossed "the line." The **GANGS** that enforced our street boundaries then were **the city council, the police department and the mayor's office.** And often now, they still are.

We were bullied into "knowing our place." We were bullied into behaving, and speaking to the majority population in a "certain" and demeaning manner. We may no longer be "segregated" by law but I suggest that we are still "segregated" to a large degree by custom and practice.

I further suggest that we are now becoming more and more segregated **by economics**. We are being **bullied** by the banks, the insurance companies, the mortgage companies and all the many other corporations. **We**, personally, are **redlined** for economic discrimination. **Our communities** are **redlined** for economic discrimination. Our groceries, gas, mortgage interest rates, auto interest rates, and other essentials seem to always cost more in our communities, than others. We are being **threatened/bullied** with **economic terrorism**. Our physical/financial well-being is being covertly threatened by the corporations. We are and have been a part of the 99% long before the S . . . hit everyone else.

I write this letter to my Bully, American Corporations, and I begin by recommending the following as our way to stand up and fight back:

The Koch Brothers are one corporation that is investing its funds into the elimination of Barack Obama as our President who supports imposing **regulations** on corporations. They are infamous in their support of the Tea Party principle of **"getting our country back"** which I interrupt as their glorious **1950's mentality** as exhibited in the movie "The Help," their nostalgic "good ole days" that I painfully lived through as a Colored, Negro, Afro-American, Black and now African America living in America.

You may want to boycott their products:

Industry/Georgia-Pacific Products, Angel Soft toilet paper, Brawny paper towels, Dixie plates, bowls, napkins and cups, Mardi Gras napkins and towels, Quilted Northern toilet paper, Soft and Gentle toilet paper, Sparkle napkins, Vanity fair napkins, Zee napkins.

Cheryl Lewis Beverly

32. Christopher Soden

the hand i was dealt

i knew you in halls and tawdry yellow gloss

of first school days ashen sky of recess

before i understood words like *queer sissy faggot*

bruiser too cool for smarts while i failed

to comprehend the history of our transaction:

fathers conferring failure upon sons and sons

transmitting futility to other sons of living

up to our dicks repugnance of thinking

another boy had anything for you the hand

withdrawn the other lad forever backing away

smiling you spat the words of estrangement

before realizing i had made some kind of choice

i might say the clock and personal witness

have only vindicated me though what to make

of your clammy paw priming my languid manhood

under god's cold mercury vapor angels

in parking lot of cruise park and rest

stop i could not begin to say

33. Monica Anderson

TRIAGE: Crisis in Community in the Form of LGBTQ Domestic Abuse

Part One: Le Petit Mort (translation: the little death) and the Under Cover Criminal

Too lightly she traipsed and tossed her snake eyes
in tattered patches of pale concealment and conscious conceit

Too boldly she built her bittersweet lies
to wield her desperate goal of destruction and deadly deceit

Too casually she laid her language of languid love
upon the warm wanton unwitting and illicit innocence of we

Too toughly she tossed her tepid tongue and yellowed teeth
to gnash at grayed ghosts - long laid bone bare at her freakish fare
fallacy

To what end is this malice made merry?
To what depths will her cruel mimicry dig deep?
In which woman will she play out her madness?
Upon what heart will she crooked crash and creep?

Her tone is one of denial
Her laughter oozes acrid disdain
Her fingers claw at blood openings
and only the raw truth will remain...

Part: Two
Momentum Stalled

Silence hung between us
like double paned security glass
our love seen and not felt
Shattered with
a
slap

I wait to go forward
I look up
for love's
divine intervention
and am met with

the deluge of push
punch
pull
pussy
pain
pulse

soon even succor seems senseless
and pride proves provoking

shards of why
slump
then
slumber
slumber
slumber

Part: Three - the Finale
Killing Spirit

Metamorph

Morpha
silicone slick sick schtick
making metamorph stick
molasses
thick venous valentine vacant

we recall our days of
torment at the hands of bullies
in school yards
and bus stops
now board rooms

we lick our wounds
in our wonderland
of shredded
love
and tether
ourselves
to this
sad old distraught
therapy

we purge upon one another

one - to - one
ominous
omni us

becoming
the bully in bed
transitioning
regurgitating
a deep pain
of a thousand love lashes
of condemnation

and distress

womb weary
we kneel
at the base of each
others altars and
crisscross our hearts
in a flutter of hope
to fly

34. Audrey F. Liggins

I was the smart kid.

I wore thick glasses by the time I was in 2nd grade because, because my grades were dropping like a stone, someone finally noticed that I couldn't see. I think I was seven the first time I was called "Four-Eyes".

I loved to read. In fact, I considered books my friends. I didn't really have many friends outside of school. I didn't really notice, or really care, that I spent most of my days indoors reading…or outside reading…or sitting in our crabapple tree…reading.

Yeah, I knew some of the kids in the neighborhood didn't like that I was smart. I thought they were stupid. They didn't like talking to adults. I liked talking with the grownups about what I read in the news or saw on television or heard on the radio because it was about the world, and the world was important to me because I knew I would travel someday. Especially given that so many people were so mad about the war going on, and my Dad was in the military.

There was a girl that lived around the corner from me.

Her name was Myra Monk. The other kids called her "Myra Monkey". I never knew why nobody liked Myra, all I knew was that she liked to read too, and so she and I were friends. Her mom was nice too, and would let Myra come over to my house after school sometimes. My mom would make us sandwiches and we'd watch television or go outside and sit in the tree, reading.

My friendship with Myra changed because, all of a sudden, the other kids started making fun of me. There were a couple of them, James and a girl whose name I now don't remember, who started following me home from school, calling me names and throwing rocks. I was a bit of a tomboy as well, so I just threw rocks back at them. None of them ever landed but they got the message that I was willing to hurt them back if I had to. Eventually, I found that more and more kids were making fun of me. I still don't know why they did it, but I found out that it was because of Myra when one of the other girls told me I would have more friends if I stopped being Myra's friend. Because nobody liked her. And I didn't know why.

What possessed me to take that advice I still can't articulate. On the one hand I didn't care that the other kids thought I was a smarty-pants, because I was. On the other hand, it really hurt me that I wasn't popular because of my choice of friends. I still don't know why. What I know for certain, is that I stopped being Myra's friend. Not only that, but I began to treat her like the other kids did.

James and the other girl whose name I can't remember, as it turned out, used to follow Myra home and throw rocks at her, just like they had done to me. Now I assume that when Myra and I became friends they stopped harassing her because now she had a witness. Regardless of why, when they began following me home they didn't expect that I would throw rocks back, because nobody else had done so before then. I learned that, if I would just treat Myra the same way all the other kids did, that I was more popular. Popularity had never been an issue before for me, and I still don't understand why it became one then. Either way, I began to harass Myra just like everyone else did.

I started calling her "Myra Monkey", just like everyone else at school did. I stopped walking home from school with her, and no, she couldn't come over to watch television or read. In retrospect it made no sense at all, because I still liked Myra. Nonetheless, I had to treat her like the other kids did, because it made me more popular.

I still feel shame when I think of Myra. It was weak of me to succumb to peer pressure. Especially so much so that I turned my back on someone who had done nothing to hurt me. Worse, I treated her abusively. Myra's family moved away shortly after that. The neighborhood was filled with military families so that was not unusual. I never got to apologize to her, or fix the relationship I had broken.

Worse, Myra told my mom what I had done. The pain the expression on my mother's face when she looked at me elicited still kills me even now, more than forty years later. I can't say that I would do things differently were I able to do it all again, but I hope that my elementary-school self would turn out to be someone who makes better choices, and has the strength to stand by her friend when her friend needs her most.

Ifalade Ta'Shia Asanti and Azaan Kamau

AFTERWORD

Azaan Kamau

Nationwide Bullying Statistics

Every 7 minutes a child is bullied; 85% of the time, there is no intervention of any kind

Each day, 160,000 students miss school due to bullying

The number one reason for suicide ages 11-16 yrs is bullying

By age 24, 60% of bullies have been charged with a crime

34% of all children report being bullied regularly at least several times a year

86% of children age 12-15 report at least some form of bullying has interfered with their studies moderately or severely

43% of middle school children avoid the bathroom and locker rooms at all costs due to certainty of being bullied

1 out of every 4 children is more than occasionally cyber-bullied

More 25 million families are currently traumatized by bullying in the U.S. today

When polled, 98% of students indicated that they want teachers to intervene

Boys who are bullies are nearly four times as likely as non-bullies to grow up to physically or sexually abuse their female partners according to a 2011 Harvard School of Health Study

In schools where there are bullying programs bullying is reduced by 50%.

Bullying was a factor in 2/3 of the 37 school shootings reviewed by the US Secret Service.

Recent bullying studies have found that schools that had a more intense bullying atmosphere, passing rates on standardized tests in such subjects as algebra, earth science and world history were 3% to 6% lower.

These statistics are way too high! We must come together to tackle the issue at the source. Why are these bullies and tormentors behaving in this manner? What is happening in their household?

Sources: stopbullying.gov, safeyouth.org, howtostopbullying.com, nmsa.org; bullypolice.org, bullybeware.com.

National Suicide Prevention Lifeline 1-800-273-TALK (8255)

ABOUT THE EDITORS

Ifalade Ta'Shia Asanti:

Is an award-winning writer, poet, journalist, TV producer and filmmaker. The author of three books, Ta'Shia continues to pen fiction that she hopes will facilitate critical thinking in conjunction with what she calls, "juicy fiction." Recipient of the Audre Lorde Black Quill Award for Creating Positive Images of Black Women in the Arts, the award for Best Contemporary Fiction by a Woman of Color and the Urban Spectrum Media Award for Outstanding Achievement in the Field of Journalism, Ta'Shia's newest book delves into the very fabric of love and its richly diverse expressions. Also look for Ta'Shia's new Talk Show airing on Your World TV, The Window, which uses social commentary to explore the issues at the forefront of global culture. More about Ta'Shia's work can be found at www.tashiaasanti.com

http://www.tashiaasanti.com

Azaan Kamau:

Azaan Kamau is an Award winning nationally syndicated journalist, poet, independent publisher, radio show producer and photographer. Azaan's work has been included in a host of other publications which include, STUD Magazine, Sinister Wisdom, The Urban Spectrum, Art Angel; Soft Stud and Other Stories, Studz Magazine and many others. Azaan has also been nominated for several awards! Azaan uses her art and writing as tools for the empowerment of all people. Azaan believes through knowledge and understanding there is no force that can oppress us. Azaan recently wrote and publishing the future New York Times Best Seller, and the internationally renowned Got Homophobia!

http://www.amazon.com/Got-Homophobia-Azaan-Kamau/dp/0615511902/ref=sr_1_1?ie=UTF8&qid=1343759742&sr=8-1&keywords=got+homophobia
http://www.azaankamau.webs.com
http://gloverlanepress.webs.com

Author's Notes:

A.H. Scott is a writer based in New York. She's a new voice and vision of fiction who has been writing short stories and poetry ever since childhood. But, now she's dipping her toe into the pond of publishing. Her writing and art is just an extension of the passion she feels for living. Every day alive can bring something new into one being's heart and soul. Art can change the world. Be it through words, or images. Sometimes, a mixture of both can get a person to think and ponder the larger meaning of being beyond just the skin which we all live within. It could be something as simple as a single tear on a beach. Or, maybe it can be as enormous as the universe beyond the stars. It all depends on where you sit in your own psyche. A.H. Scott is author of two novels, "Over My Head" and "Rack Em". Also she has several short stories (FREE and nominally priced) from Smashwords, Amazon, Barnes & Noble, and iTunes. A.H. SCOTT LINKS -
http://www.twitter.com/ahscottnyc
http://www.facebook.com/ahscottnycdiamond
http://www.soundclick.com/ahscott
http://ahscottnyc.angelfire.com/index.html
http://musingpastthefuture.blogspot.com/

Amy La Coe holds an M.A. Education Counseling, June 1993, California State University, Dominguez Hills. M.A. Sociology, December 1977, University of California, Los Angeles. Academic Counselor and Human Development Counselor at El Camino College, Torrance, CA 90506 1995 to Present.   Also an Academic Counselor at Cerritos College and Long Beach City College. A trans-woman who went full-time in 2007 and had gender reassignment surgery in 2011.

April Mae Berza is a member of Poetic Genius Society. She always has a kindred spirit with a wide scope of imagination. Her poems

and short stories appeared in Maganda Magazine, Remembering Rizal: Voices from the Diaspora, KAAL Episcopal Literature and 2012 VAANI anthology. She is the author of Berso de Berza (Charging Ram, 2012). She lives in the Philippines.
http://www.chargingram.com/aprilmaeberza.html
http://poeticgenius.org/tag/april-mae-m-berza/

Aser Peleg... Dolphin / Cherub / Bakla Poet

http://www .feygeleah.blogspot.com/2011/12/chewing-gum-bukkake.html or
http://shechinotown.weebly.com/2/post/2012/07/wilderness-generation.html

Audrey F. Liggins is Ms. Audrey the radio personality of Ms. Audrey's House! Ms. Audrey is an entrepreneur, talk show host and CEO of Ms. Audrey's House, LLC! Visit her and give her a listen at http://www.msaudreyshouse.com

Christopher Soden is a native Texan. He is a writer, teacher, critic, lecturer and performer. Christopher received his MFA in Writing (Poetry) from Vermont College in January of 2005. He's taught classes and guest lectured on the subjects of craft, theory, genre, literature and publication. He currently writes theatre critique for Examiner.com, PegasusNews.com, and A + C DFW. He has written poetry, plays, performance pieces, literary, film and theatre critique. His first poetry collection, Closer, was released by Rebel Satori/Queer Mojo : June 14th, 2011. His honors include: Full Fellowship for Lambda Literary Retreat: Emerging LGBT Voices August 2010. Distinguished Poets of Dallas, Poetry Society of America's Poetry in Motion Series, Founding Member, President and President Emeritus of The Dallas Poets Community. Finalist in Dobie Paisano Fellowship, 4Th Unity and LSU Outworks Drama Festivals. Finalist in Robin Becker and Refined Savage Chapbook Contests. His work has appeared in : Collective Brightness, Resilience, Assaracus, The Q Review, A Face to Meet the Faces,

Ganymede Poets : One, Gay City 2, The Café Review, The Texas Observer, Sentence, Borderlands, Off the Rocks, The James White Review, The New Writer, Velvet Mafia, Poetry Super Highway, Gertrude, Touch of Eros, Gents, Bad Boys and Barbarians, Windy City Times, ArLiJo, Best Texas Writing 2.
https://www.facebook.com/pages/Closer/231817783495638?ref=ts

Denina Taylor is a passionate writer of poetry, prose, and short stories. Denina is also passionate about the weather! She studies storm patterns, cloud formations, climate temperature, as if she was her own meteorologist and forecaster! Currently Denina is an IT Student and a parent of a 14 year old daughter. Denina has a wonderful partner who has stuck by her side through the thick, and the thin. Denina is currently working on her first novel "Blood Relatives", as well as a lesbian erotica anthology

DJ Nova Jade is an award-winning DJ + independent film producer. Also a published writer and poet, Tera* has blogged with the Jewish Journal's "Oy Gay" blog since 2010. When she isn't creating art, she engages in social justice activism on a local and national level and is a social entrepreneur with a global focus. DJ Nova Jade is also on of the featured contributors of the best seller STUD; Dispelling The Myths by Azaan Kamau. Follow her on twitter @djnovajade and all other social networks under '/djnovajade', with a listing on Beatport at http://dj.beatport.com/djnovajade http://tera.wakeupnow.com.

Ed Madden is the author of two books of poetry: *Signals*, which won the 2007 South Carolina Poetry Book Prize, and *Prodigal: Variations*. His work also appears in *Best New Poets 2007*, *Best Gay Poetry 2008*, and the Notre Dame anthology *The Book of Irish American Poetry*. He lives in South Carolina. His poetry has been previously published in *Assaracus*."

Gary Dixon was born in Sedalia, Missouri, appropriately in the middle 70's--the "Me Decade." Two weeks premature and three pounds underweight, he had a strong desire to to overcome a life confined to an incubator. Perhaps this tenacity, from his very start, is the best metaphor for his life. Gary's love for the written word was well established as a child, reading for hours on end, in his own little world. By age six, he would take stories from his favorite book, "My Book of Bible Stories," and perform them as newscasts to the annoyance of family, friends and to all who were in the vicinity.

Gary's own interest in writing really didn't manifest until he discovered the works of Essex Hemphill in his teens. His interest further was reinforced later in his 20s, through association with Sojolity Prime, a phenomenal woman and writer who would become his 'bestie' for life. Both Hemphill and Prime inspired Gary to explore ideas regarding life, love, trials and all else on his own terms--as a Black, same gender loving (SGL) individual. Prime provided significant encouragement to craft his artistry further, as well. He never has looked back!

Gary officially came out of the spoken word performance closet a little over two years ago, when he worked up the nerve to attend a weekly open mic event in the neighborhood in which he resided. A resident of Columbus, Ohio, he continues to explore writing while taking poetry and other classes at The Ohio State University and working on his open mic presentation at various clubs around the city, using the nom de plume "sinnawitsoul." Writing and performing are ways by which Gary works out his own insecurities about who he as a Black SGL man, hopefully making it easier for those who are coming after him to lighten their loads and know their worth is in the community at large.

Also a quiet activist, Gary is a founding member of an LGBTQ affirming Christian ministry, The RESTORATION Church (Columbus), where he serves in a leadership capacity. He is excited about the work that they are destined to do, as LGBTQ persons strive to heal the hurts suffered at the hands of the Church and by religious people. Gary is honored that his piece "Are You Happy Now" has been included within this amazing and timely anthology that is addressing one of the many issues that continues to plague our community. He can be reached via Facebook @ www.facebook.com/sinnawitsoul.

Jacquelyn Kennedy is an entrepreneur, visionary, philanthropist and author. She is also one of the founders of the Dewberries Cultural Center.
http://www.luvthatdewberries.com/cultural_center

Jasper Odasor is a New York City based essayist, poet and fiction writer. He is currently working on a historical fiction novel exploring eroticism and spirituality across many cultures. "You Throw Like A girl!" is part of a larger body ofwork.Soulwrite@hotmail.com

Jazar F. Kahr Poet and Author of 3 books and 1 upcoming book! http://www.jazarkahr.webs.com

Jessica Knapp... I am a strong and powerful woman in recovery, carrying a message of peace... I have been on a self improvement path since September 9, 1984 when the pain of remaining the same was greater than the fear of change...

 I have found great healing in my writing, and as it turns out, so have others...

 My life's purpose is to give back freely what has been given to me. I do this by sharing without regret, shame, or censorship my experience, strength & hope in my writing, knowing there are countless others finding their own healing within my pages.

 I can be found writing my next book somewhere in sunny northern California, in the Bay Area, typing happily next to my wife. Nearby, either putting their noses on the keyboard or sleeping on my lap is our miniature dachshund family.

My first book called More Will Be Revealed.... One Glimpse At A Time will be published before the end of 2012. Look for it on my website jessiesync.com

I am currently working on my second book.

KATRINA…Author Katrina, known as "The Lesbian Love Doctor" is the best selling author of over 18 books on lesbian love, dating & relationships, erotica and spirituality. Katrina???s focus is on building and maintaining healthy, lasting, loving lesbian relationships. She is also looking forward to setting up workshops in the very near future, which will be for both single lesbians and couples, on a myriad of topics; including love and mystical sex retreats, esoteric spirituality and African spirituality. She is highly intuitive, has studied astrology for over 20 years and is also available for astrological or other types of spiritual readings. On the Love Magic novel official web site you'll find excerpt's from both Love Magic and Spellbound, the novel's sexy companion handbook! Also available on the site is the Love Magic store. You can purchase clothing, accessories, home decor and other gifts with cool logo's like "Sexy Witch", "Voodoo Rockstar", "Creole Princess", "I put A Spell On You", "Voodoo Queen" and more! Katrina also offers New Orleans style Hoodoo Lessons for download! Love Magic and Spellbound were created out of Katrina's love for New Orleans and it's rich history and connection to her African ancestors. When you open the pages of this book, you'll be transported to a world of mystery, passion, desire and erotic power! www.lovemagicnovel.webs.com www.thelesbianbadgirl.webs.com

Kevin McLellan is the author of the chapbook Round Trip (Seven Kitchens, 2010), a collaborative series of poems with numerous women poets. He has recent or forthcoming poems in journals including: Barrow Street, Colorado Review, failbetter, Horse Less Review, Kenyon Review Online, Sixth Finch, Western Humanities Review, Witness and numerous others. Kevin lives in Cambridge MA, and sometimes teaches poetry workshops at the University of Rhode Island in Providence.
https://sites.google.com/site/kevinmclellanpoetry/

Kergan Edwards-Stout is an award-winning director, screenwriter, and author, and recently published his debut novel, SONGS FOR THE NEW DEPRESSION. He is honored to have been named one of the Human Rights Campaign's 2011 Fathers of the Year and blogs regularly at http://kerganedwards-stout.com

Monica Anderson, MA, PhD abd is a community member, parent, strategist, writer, journalist, curator, producer, and project manager committed to transformation and pro-activism. Her founding developments include Kinfolkz, Sista2Sista, OMNI: the Bi/Pan/Trans Women and Transmen of Color Network and SankofaEvents.com. These organizations are nationally recognized vehicles for sociopolitical transformation that embody Monica's affinity for supporting LGBTQIA family empowerment, identifying sustainable community resources, and encouraging education through the creative arts and live performance. From 2010 to present, Monica has successfully co-produced the internationally recognized and widely attended Oakland Pride festival (estimated attendance 50,000 celebrants). Monica's project management skills set has drawn clients from all over the globe and has taken her to places like: Tokyo, Japan; Cape Town South Africa; Madrid, Spain; Amsterdam, Netherlands; and Jamaica, West Indies. She works closely with individuals, city officials, community organizations and county agencies to enhance countless projects through her management, strategic design and related project coordination: SF Pride, The Water for Haiti Project, The Green Festival, The Ayiti Resurrect Fundraiser, Sweet Water: Celebrating Queer Black Female Heritage, The Oakland LGBT Roundtable, FIERCE NYC, Focus Features film premieres of PARIAH, The Rhythms Sistas Healing Drum Circle, The IAmPariahToo campaign, Stanford University Splash Education, The East Bay Queer Women's Book Discussion Group and more. http://www.SankofaEvents.com, http://www.mykinfolkz.com and http://www.mySista2Sista.com

Neil Ellis Orts is a writer and performer currently living in Houston, Texas. He writes fiction as well as articles on religion and art, and has been published both locally and nationally. He recently places his first comic book script for, coincidentally, an anti-bullying comic called Voices Against Bullying, to be published in late 2012 by Sword and Labrys Productions. Active blogs: Crumbs at the Feast http://crumbsatthefeast.blogspot.com/ me kissing you http://mekissingyou.blogspot.com/

Ona Marae is a Queer Femme living, loving and writing in Denver, Colorado. She is a Disability/ LGBTQ Rights activist as well as a Pastor in a progressive Christian Church and loves to talk integrating spirituality and sexuality. She has known bullies inside and outside her family since she can remember and is proud to be a part of this anthology. It might have changed her life back then. She knows it will change lives now.

Rab Marlow is a writer, artist and clown who lives on 18 wooded acres in rural Indiana with his husband Dave where they raise chickens and flowers. Rab's work has been anthologized and has appeared in The Sun, White Crane Journal and RFD, among others. He is a monthly columnist for The Community Letter, believed to be the country's oldest LGBT newspaper in continuous publication. He blogs at gayfeather.blogspot.com

R. D. Wylder is a freelancer, poet, and fan of the written word. She started writing in her teens, thus far amassing a collection of over 200 poems, articles and short stories. She has recently been published in Off The Rocks: Volume 15. Currently located in the Caribbean, she can usually be found tinkering with her websites. www.rdwylder.com www.eeriewhispers.com

Rebecca A. Raymer is a writer and author living in her hometown of Atlanta, Georgia. Her first novel, Light through the Cracks, has been downloaded over 30,000 times, and was the #1 Fiction and the #1 Overall novel for June 2012 on free-ebooks.net. Rebecca's childhood was filled with rape, torture, incest, sexual slavery, and other forms of abuse and exploitation. Her adulthood is filled with love and strength, and in addition to writing, she advocates to expose people who sexually assault children now, who have sexually assaulted children in the past, and anyone who has looked the other way when a child has been harmed. Her blog, Putting it ALL Out There (http://puttingitallouthere.blogspot.com/), is a brutally honest and controversial expression of Rebecca's experiences as an adult recovering from the horrors of her childhood. Please visit www.rebeccaaraymer.com to contact Rebecca, learn more about her, get a FREE copy of her novel, check out her blogs, and find information about resources and organizations that are awesome.

Shannon Pacaoan holds a BA in Psychology and in Asian American Studies from San Francisco State University. Recognizing the unique healing properties of art within her community, she has come to believe in the transformative power of art for both artist and audience. She has since dedicated much of her time to help others bring their unique stories to stage in the Bay Area with Asian American Theater Company (AATC), Bindlestiff Studio, Kearny Street Workshop, Kularts, Pinays Maintaining Sisterhood Through Art and Revival Arts Productions.

She has worked both backstage — on AATC's 15th Anniversary Production of *Walls* (2006), awarded a National Endowment for the Arts (NEA) grant — and on stage with her script "Circadian Suites", featured in Pinays Maintaining Sisterhood Through Art's production, *Death of a Player* (2011), the recipient of a Zellerbach Family Foundation grant.

Her most extensive work is found in The Bakla Show (Co-creator/Producer) which aims to educate, challenge, and encourage dialogue among and between different ethnic and sexually diverse communities by means of increasing the visibility of Filipino American LGBTQ/GNC experience through theatrical performance. Read more at *thebaklashow.wordpress.com*.

Currently based on the Central Coast of California, she continues to seek new ways to engage her community through storytelling, speaking on the panel 'Sticks and Stones: Bullying in School and Community in San Luis Obispo' (2011).

Tammy L. R. Young is the founder and brain-child behind the Confessions & Expressions Journal Collection. Tammy has been writing and creating since child hood and has been published in the Tapestries of Faith: SGLBT African American Stories of Faith, Love & Family anthology .

Tammy is the proud Mom of the **The Henderson Sisters** visit Tammy at: http://www.blurb.com/user/store/tammy_young

http://urbanlyfestylesmagazine.com/profile/TammyYoung

Tim M. West! Black, gay-identified, feminist, POZ, and working class, Tim'm T. West has embraced all of who he is and, with laser-beam precision, harnessed the power of his truth to illuminate, celebrate, inspire, provoke, and bear witness. As a teacher, performance artist, author, and culture producer, Tim'm has become an exemplar among contemporary Renaissance personalities of the early 21st Century as he brings others to voice through education for critical consciousness. Indeed, that Tim'm has been interviewed by such dizzying array of media outlets from Newsweek to the New York Times is a testament to his importance to the spirit and history of the times as a foundational maverick among black, multi-disciplinary artists. Even a restricted Google' search of just his name yields thousands of Internet occurrences. The foundation for Tim'm's work as an Educator and Scholar can be found in the red dirt of Taylor, Arkansas where Tim'm grew up before leaving for Duke University where he completed his BA. http://www.reddirt.biz

Tina Cates, Poet name Dyvacat started writing in her teenage years which consisted of poetry and songs. She latter began an online poetry group that pushed her into expanding her poetry onto the stage. She has performed her pieces for Sappho?s Return, Out Fest Film Festival, The Found Theatre in Long Beach, Ca. and several other venues across Southern Ca., New York and in Sacramento where she currently resides. She is the Author of Spoken Wordz and Kitty Kat Letters. Dedication: This book is dedicated to my two highest blessings, my children Raina and Xavier Cates. Push for your Dreams and they will Come True!! Love Momma! Kitty Kat Letters Dedication: I dedicate this book to the freedom of Self Expression and Discovery! ?Let the Evolution Continue!!? Find Her On Facebook!

Tiffany C. Pace....For more than 10 years, Tiffany C. Pace, also known as Poetic Old Soul, has been writing poetry & has performed spoken word at open mic events in the East Bay, CA, which includes Listen & Be Heard, 3rd Eye Collective Presents: Life Sentence, Oakland Poetry Slam & Open Mic, to name a few.

She has shared her poetry at Sistahfest, as well as the NIA Gathering, both retreats for same-gender loving women of African descent in CA. In September of 2009, Tiffany released her self-published, handmade, poetry book debut entitled "Versatility: Introducing Poetic Old Soul". On the same month, she made her feature debut at Butch 'N Nellie's in Sacramento, CA. She has participated in poetry slam competitions and won 3rd place at Life Sentence, but Tiffany's heart has always been open mic poetry, for she prefers the audience to feel her passionate words. Tiffany has also shared her poetry on Blog Talk Radio's Blood, Sweat & Tears, Allways Open Mic, and Eryk Moore's Verbal Ink.

Tiffany continues to write poetry, perform at open mic poetry events in the East Bay & lives comfortably in Fairfield, CA.

Please visit Tiffany's websites at:
http://www.facebook.com/PoeticOldSoul
http://www.youtube.com/poeticoldsoul

Tom Rastrelli enjoys writing across the genres. Currently, he is finishing a memoir about his journey into and out of the Catholic priesthood. He's a 2011 graduate of the University of Southern California's Master of Professional Writing program. While there, he was a finalist in the USC MPW Writing for Stage and Screen Festival and a scholarship recipient for the New York State Summer Writers Institute. His work has been published in Aunt Chloe, Colere, and The Huffington Post http://www.huffingtonpost.com/tom-rastrelli/ His blog, www.gospelaccordingtohate.com, confronts religious hypocrisy with a mixture of memoir, commentary, and personal essay. Tom has a B.A. in Theatre Arts from the University of Northern Iowa and a Master of Divinity from St. Mary's Seminary & University, Baltimore. He is proud of his native Iowa, where he recently returned to marry his husband, Bruce

Yolanda Arroyo Pizarro is an award winning Puerto Rican writer author of novels Caparazones (2010), and Los documentados published in Puerto Rico and Spain. She also won the National Institute of Puerto Rican Literature Prize in 2008, the Woman Latino Writer Award Residency from National Hispanic Culture Center in Albuquerque, New Mexico in 2011 and the PEN Club Prize on 2010 and 2006. Arroyo Pizarro is the Director of Puerto Rican writers participating in the Puerto Rican Word Festival attended in Old San Juan and New York. She teaches Survival Creative Writing Workshops in San Juan, PR for victims and survivors of domestic violence. Blog http://narrativadeyolanda.blogspot.com/ and Twitter https://twitter.com/YArroyoPizarro

Very Special Thanks to Authors:

Bill Klemm

Cheryl Lewis Beverly

Jeremy Halinen

Lindsay Delong

Rachel Towns

Scott Taylor